AIR CAMPAIGN

DESERT STORM 1991

The most shattering air campaign in history

RICHARD P. HALLION | ILLUSTRATED BY ADAM TOOBY

OSPREY PUBLISHING
Bloomsbury Publishing Plc
Kemp House, Chawley Park, Cumnor Hill, Oxford OX2 9PH, UK
29 Earlsfort Terrace, Dublin 2, Ireland
1385 Broadway, 5th Floor, New York, NY 10018, USA
E-mail: info@ospreypublishing.com
www.ospreypublishing.com

OSPREY is a trademark of Osprey Publishing Ltd

First published in Great Britain in 2022

A catalogue record for this book is available from the British Library.

ISBN: PB 9781472846969; eBook: 9781472846976
ePDF: 9781472846945; XML: 9781472846952

22 23 24 25 26 10 9 8 7 6 5 4 3 2 1

Maps by bounford.com
Diagrams by Adam Tooby
3D BEVs by Paul Kime
Index by Alan Rutter
Typeset by PDQ Digital Media Solutions, Bungay, UK
Printed and bound in India by Replika Press Private Ltd.

To find out more about our authors and books visit www.ospreypublishing.com. Here
you will find extracts, author interviews, details of forthcoming events and the option to
sign up for our newsletter.

Author's dedication:
In fond remembrance of Air
Commodore Jeremy J. "Jerry" Witts
RAF DSO FRAeS ADC 1950–2020,
an outstanding strike pilot, inspirational
leader, and treasured friend who flew
and commanded Vulcan, Buccaneer, and
Tornado squadrons and detachments,
excelling in all he did. His skill,
dedication, and extraordinary good
humor were exceeded only by his
steadfastness and great personal courage.

AIR CAMPAIGN

CONTENTS

INTRODUCTION

December 22, 1989: Standing on the infamous Berlin Wall, East and West Berliners celebrate the collapse of the East German state and the reunification of the two Germanys. (Department of Defense (DoD))

In the last years of the Cold War, while the Soviet Union tottered towards collapse, the first major conflict of the post-Cold War era was brewing in the Persian Gulf. After the bloodbath of the Iran–Iraq War ended in a ceasefire, an illusory peace lasted not quite two years. By war's end Iraq had greatly expanded its military forces, drawing its arms from both the West and East, but most notably France, the Soviet Union, and China. Bankrolled largely by the Gulf states, it now possessed the world's fourth largest army and the sixth largest air force, with robust armoured, artillery, and missile forces. With Iran temporarily neutralized, Saddam Hussein – unwilling to pay his war debts to the Gulf Cooperation Council and coveting oil-rich Kuwait, invaded that tiny country on August 2, 1990.

In response, the United States, Britain, and Saudi Arabia shaped and built a global coalition, pouring in troops and materiel in preparation for a high-technology and high-tempo war that, for scope and scale, eerily recollected NATO's 1980 plans for confronting the Warsaw Pact's massive armoured, air, and missile forces in Europe.

While strenuous diplomatic negotiations and successive United Nations (UN) resolutions failed to get Saddam Hussein to withdraw his troops from Kuwait, armchair critics predicted disaster should the Coalition attack dug-in Iraqi forces in Kuwait. "Such an offensive, even if successful, would be long and costly," wrote commentators in *The Baltimore Sun*, "entailing thousands and perhaps tens of thousands of American casualties." Even a retired US Army Chief of Staff, Gen Edward C. "Shy" Meyer, predicted up to 30,000 killed, wounded, and missing. Those extolling the merits of air power came in for special criticism, with economist and public intellectual John Kenneth Galbraith archly proclaiming "there's no issue to be regarded with such doubt as this."

With diplomatic efforts exhausted, the Coalition went to war on January 17, 1991, quickly shattering Iraq's military and forcing its withdrawal from Kuwait after 43 days. The key to victory was evident from the first minutes of conflict: the Coalition's overwhelming air power employed by its air forces, navies, and armies.

Over the course of the war, fixed- and rotary-wing air power (informed and enhanced by reconnaissance aircraft, electronic intelligence collectors, and orbiting space systems furnishing intelligence, warning, weather, communications, and navigation) devastated Iraq's integrated air defense system (IADS); shattered its Air Force as an effective fighting arm; disrupted and persistently hindered effective command and control; prosecuted round-the-clock air attacks that pinned Iraqi troops in place; cut key rail and road links, thus denying them meaningful resupply; reduced fielded armour and artillery strength by direct air attack; frustrated (though it did not end) employment of theater-ranging ballistic missiles and battlefield rocket artillery; and demoralized soldiers so greatly that many contemplated killing their officers, others deserted (risking summary execution if found by Saddam's enforcement squads), and some even took their own lives rather than endure what had become for them an unbearable ordeal of round-the-clock air attacks.

When Coalition ground forces breached Iraqi defenses to cross into Iraq and Kuwait, Coalition air power greatly facilitated their assault. In four days, the Coalition liberated Kuwait, seized 28,500 square miles of territory, and took over 87,000 Iraqi POWs. Combat concluded with a ceasefire at 0800hrs on February 28, and a truce at Safwan on March 3, 1991 ended the war. By then Iraq's army had shrunk from the world's fourth largest to Iraq's fourth largest. Victory came at the price of 341 Coalition dead, and 776 Coalition wounded.

The air campaign plan reflected the bitter lessons and experience of Vietnam and the Middle East wars, coupled with an appreciation of what new technologies afforded: routine precision attack so that air strategists could plan in terms of number of targets destroyed per sortie, not numbers of sorties to destroy a particular target; stealthy strikes via the very low observable (VLO) radar signature F-117; space-based intelligence, navigation, communication, warning, and weather; airborne battle management and air-space deconfliction; and global-ranging mobility (and combat operations) via a "tanker bridge." By emphasizing *simultaneous, parallel* war rather than *sequential, linear* war (as in previous air campaigns), air planners – working at the direction of Lt Gen Charles "Chuck" Horner, the coalition's air commander – left Iraq's airmen and air defenders both overwhelmed and on the defensive, unable to protect their ground forces in Kuwait or even the air space and territory of Iraq itself. While there were "wild cards" – appalling weather, missile strikes against Israel and Saudi Arabia, the battle of al-Khafji, an enervating intelligence brouhaha in mid-campaign, and the al-Firdos bunker bombing – none derailed the campaign, nor kept it from achieving its purposes.

Desert Storm's air campaign marked the first time in military history in which air power was used as the lead force – the veritable centerpiece – in the strategy and execution of a war. As such, it radically redirected thinking about air power and its employment, evident in postwar doctrinal changes in many global militaries. It validated having a theater commander with reporting co-equal (if interdependent) air, land, and maritime component commanders, each possessing tasking authority across their respective air, land, and sea Coalition forces. It heralded as well a new era: routine precise, discrete, simultaneous, parallel, and diffuse attack from above.

The campaign plan emphasized nodal, effects-based warfare – using the power of precision attack to reduce key Iraqi capabilities, not simply striking at sequential target lists or randomly bombing population centers. By not opting for a "body-count"-driven model of war emphasizing the punishing attritional clash of massed land forces, planners created a campaign that produced (by previous standards) mercifully low casualties to both attacker and defender, a characteristic of other air-dominant wars since then.

It was, in short, war according to Sun Tzu, not Clausewitz. Military analysts, war college cognoscenti, and historians continue to debate whether (as some have said, including this author) that it constituted a "Revolution in Military Affairs" (RMA). But that it transformed perceptions, expectations, doctrine, strategy, and employment of air power is beyond doubt.

CHRONOLOGY

1988

20 August The Iraq–Iran war ends with a United Nations-brokered cease-fire.

1989

February Iraq, North Yemen, Jordan, and Egypt form the Arab Cooperation Council (ACC), which the Saudi leadership perceives as a strategic effort orchestrated by Saddam to encircle Saudi Arabia and counter the Gulf Cooperation Council (GCC).

16 October Gen Colin Powell, Chairman of the US Joint Chiefs of Staff (CJCS), directs CENTCOM (Central Command) to prepare to defend the Arabian peninsula from Iraq. This leads to OPLAN 1002-90, the conceptual heart of Operation *Desert Storm*.

November CINCCENT (Commander-in-Chief of CENTCOM) Gen Norman Schwarzkopf and COMUSCENTAF (Commander US CENTCOM Air Forces) Lt Gen Charles Horner meet to discuss the Iraqi threat to Kuwait and also their respective responsibilities as land and air component commanders, shaping their personal relationship and future roles through the Gulf War.

1990

19 February Saddam demands the US remove its warships from the Persian Gulf.

2 April Saddam threatens to "make fire eat half of Israel if it tries anything against Iraq."

April Horner and his staff structure a three-option deterrent, defense, and offensive contingency plan to counter an Iraqi attack on Saudi Arabia.

28–30 May Saddam calls for Arabs to liberate Jerusalem and attack America.

July CENTCOM exercise *Internal Look* predicts heavy casualties if Iraq invades Kuwait and then Saudi Arabia.

22 July Saddam assures Egypt's President Hosni Mubarak he will not attack Kuwait.

25 July Saddam meets with US Ambassador April Glaspie, with each offering differing accounts of the meeting.

1 August Schwarzkopf briefs Secretary of Defense Richard Cheney and the Joint Chiefs of Staff that an Iraqi attack on Kuwait is a "certainty."

2 August Iraqi military forces invade Kuwait, triggering the Gulf crisis of 1990 and leading to the Gulf War of 1991.

British Prime Minister Margaret Thatcher tells President George H.W. Bush that "Aggressors must never be appeased."

American, British, and French naval forces begin steaming to the Gulf.

UN Security Council issues Resolution 660 condemning the invasion and demanding Iraq's withdrawal.

The *Desert Shield* build-up saw the Coalition assemble an interesting and sometimes eclectic international mix of old and new aircraft. Here, at Thumrait, Oman, in mid-August 1990, an early 1960s-vintage Hawker Hunter FR.10 reconnaissance fighter of the Sultan of Oman's Air Force (SOAF) taxis back from a sortie, passing late-1980s McDonnell-Douglas F-15E Strike Eagles of the 4th TFW's 336th TFS, while, in the far background, are a brace of SOAF 1970s SEPECAT Jaguar S(O) strike fighters. Note the Hunter two-place trainers masked by the leading F-15E. (DoD)

4 August Schwarzkopf and Joint Force Air Component Commander (JFACC), Lt Gen Horner, brief OPLAN 1002-90 to President Bush.

6 August Cheney, Schwarzkopf, and Horner persuade Saudi King Fahd to open Saudi Arabia to deploying US forces.

7 August Operation *Desert Shield* begins.

PM Thatcher orders RAF aircraft to the Gulf.

USS *Independence* (CV-62) arrives in Gulf of Oman; USS *Eisenhower* (CVN-69) is enroute to Red Sea.

8 August First US aircraft, 23 F-15Cs, land at Dhahran.

First US ground troops depart for Saudi Arabia.

9 August King Fahd appoints Gen Khaled bin Sultan Joint Force Commander (JFC), co-equivalent to CENTCOM's Schwarzkopf.

10 August Canadian PM Brian Mulroney orders a naval task force to the Gulf, expanded later to include CF-18s and support aircraft.

11 August First UK aircraft, 24 Tornado F.3s and 12 Jaguar GR.1As, arrive in Saudi Arabia.

First troops from a foreign Islamic nation (Egypt) arrive in Saudi Arabia.

12 August First contingent of B-52Gs arrive at Diego Garcia.

17 August US activates Stage I of the Civil Reserve Air Fleet (CRAF); Stage II is activated subsequently.

20 August US sends 18 F-117A stealth fighters to the Gulf, augmented by a second force in November; F-117A total strength in Gulf eventually rises to 42 aircraft.

Checkmate's Col John A. Warden III briefs *Instant Thunder* campaign concept to Horner and his staff, who retains Lt Col David A. Deptula among others to work on campaign planning. Warden thereafter employs Checkmate to support Horner's planners with quick-turn intelligence fusion and analysis.

22 August Horner appoints Brig Gen Buster Glosson as his director of campaign plans.

26 August PM Thatcher, in a telecon with President Bush, emphasizes steadfastness towards Iraq, cautioning him that now was "no time to go wobbly."

1 September Italy announces it will deploy Tornado IDSs and support aircraft to the Gulf.

6 September UK Parliament overwhelmingly approves sending forces to the Gulf.

11 September President Bush informs Congress "We will not let this aggression stand."

17 September Following a controversial media interview, Gen Michael Dugan is relieved as Air Force Chief of Staff, replaced by Gen Merrill "Tony" McPeak.

3 October First French combat aircraft arrive at Al Ahsa, Saudi Arabia.

7 October First Canadian CF-18s arrive at Doha.

11 October Glosson briefs evolved air plan to senior US leadership.

14 October Canadian CF-18s force Iraqi aircraft away from USN ships.

1 November UK Deputy PM Geoffrey Howe resigns, precipitating a distracting three-week power struggle for leadership of the Conservative Party.

8 November Bush administration announces a vastly increased deployment.

14 November Schwarzkopf briefs the land campaign plan to CENTCOM.

22 November PM Margaret Thatcher announces her resignation, a casualty of the Conservative Party's internal squabbling, leaving office on 28 November, and is replaced by PM John Major.

29 November UN Security Council issues Resolution 678 authorizing "all means necessary" to enforce previous resolutions if Iraq does not leave Kuwait by 15 January 1991.

2 December Iraq test-fires two Al-Hussein missiles.

17 December UK ACM Sir Patrick "Paddy" Hine, joint commander of Operation *Granby*, visits the Gulf, is briefed in detail on the air plan, subsequently briefing PM John Major.

1991

12 January US Congress authorizes using force to carry out UN Resolutions in Iraq.

15 January President Bush authorizes the execution of *Desert Storm*.

16–17 January Operation *Desert Storm* commences at 2339 GMT (2339Z), January 16 (0239 local January 17) with attacks by aircraft, helicopters, and cruise missiles.

18 January Iraq fires Al Hussein missiles at Israel and Saudi Arabia, beginning the so-called "Great Scud Hunt."

US Army Patriot air defense team at Dhahran shoot down an Iraqi missile with two Patriots, the first antiballistic missile kill in history.

A Saudi-based US Army missile crew launches two MGM-140A ATACMS (Army Tactical Missile System), destroying an Iraqi SA-2 site more than 60 miles distant, the first precision ballistic missile strike in history.

Operation *Proven Force* F-111Es from Incirlik, Turkey undertake their first combat operations, against four early-warning radar sites in northern Iraq.

19 January USS *Louisville* (SSN-724) becomes the first submarine in history to attack a land target with a cruise missile when it launches five TLAM-C cruise missiles against Iraq while on patrol under the Red Sea.

Navy attack aircraft first employ McDonnell-Douglas AGM-84E SLAMs (Standoff Land Attack Missiles) against Iraqi coastal targets.

The US Army deploys two Patriot batteries to Israel.

CENTAF flies Package Q against three targets in Baghdad, the war's largest strike. Unwieldy execution and the density of air defenses results in two F-16s lost to SAMs. Afterwards, CENTAF employs smaller packages and makes Baghdad off-limits to F-16s.

23 January RAF Tornados switch from low-level to medium altitude attacks.

Coalition attackers begin a "shelter-busting" program.

24 January A Saudi F-15C downs two Iraqi Mirage F-1s bound for a Saudi oil terminal.

CENTCOM detects over two dozen Iraqi aircraft crossing into Iran, the beginning of what becomes a series of desperate flights to escape to safety. In response, three F-15C patrols are established along the Iraq–Iran border.

25 January Iraq creates a massive Gulf oil spill from the al-Ahmadi refinery and oiling buoy; in response, an F-111F GBU-15 strike drastically cuts the oil flow.

27 January Coalition declares "air supremacy" over Iraq.

28 January F-4Gs and A-10s team up to destroy an SA-3 site northwest of Ali Al-Salem Air Base, Kuwait, the beginning of "Wart Weasel" SEAD operations.

29 January Joint service sea–air raid on Umm-al-Maradim by American and Kuwaiti naval and Marine forces.

UK, US, and Canadian air–sea strikes destroy the Iraqi Navy, the "Bubiyan Turkey Shoot."

The Battle of al-Khafji commences.

31 January Spirit 03, an Air Force special operations AC-130H gunship supporting Marines fighting at Khafji, is shot down by a shoulder-fired missile, killing all 14 aboard, the single greatest air combat loss of the war.

1 February In a major policy reversal, France agrees to permit British-based B-52Gs to transit through French airspace while on raids against Iraq.

2 February Striking a highway bridge north of as-Samawah, four Tornado crews make the first laser-guided bomb (LGB) attack in RAF history, cued by two Buccaneers with Pave Spike designation pods.

Schwarzkopf rejects an amphibious invasion of Kuwait.

4 February At the behest of Canadian airmen, and following discussions between Horner and Canadian officials, Canada's CF-18s are released from strictly maritime operations to fly offensive air-to-ground operations.

5 February President Bush orders Cheney, Wolfowitz, and Powell to Riyadh to assess the war; they meet with Schwarzkopf and other commanders on 8–9 February.

Battleship USS *Missouri* shells and destroys two Iraqi radar sites with its 16in main battery, marking the third war in which it engages shore targets.

First F-111F antiarmour test using night LGB attacks cued by Pave Tack; Horner hails test as "classic of how to do the job right." This marks the beginning of nightly "tank-plinking."

6 February Special Operations MC-130Es drop BLU-82 fuel-air bombs in Southern Iraq, successfully deceiving Iraqi air defenders into thinking the ground war was about to commence and who turned on all their remaining air defense radars, revealing their location to Coalition targeteers. MC-130Es drop three others on Faylakah Island later in war.

Provisional IRA undertakes a damaging mortar attack on 10 Downing Street, London, during a meeting of the War Cabinet, fortunately without inflicting casualties.

10 February First use of TIALD self-designation pods for RAF Tornado LGB drops.

12 February Photo reconnaissance reveals MiG-21bis fighters from the Iraqi Air Force's No. 14 Squadron at Abu Talib air base (Tallil) parked beside the Ziggurat of Ur, a culturally protected historical site, in a bid to ensure their survival.

13 February al-Firdos bunker strike, with hundreds of civilian casualties, leads to international outcry and restrictions on bombing within Baghdad.

24 February "G-Day," the beginning of the ground offensive.

25 February An unengaged Iraqi missile strikes Dhahran, killing 28 US Army reservists and wounding 97 others, the greatest single American loss of life in the war.

J-STARS detects Iraqi III Corps withdrawing, triggering concentrated attacks.

28 February As per a directive from President Bush, Coalition offensive operations cease at 0800L (0500Z).

3 March Schwarzkopf and Khaled meet at Safwan with Iraqi Army Vice Chief of Staff Lt Gen Sultan Hashim Ahmad al-Jabburi and Iraqi III Corps commander Maj Gen Salah Aboud Mahmoud and settle on a ceasefire.

USAF General Dynamics F-16C Fighting Falcon fighter-bombers (nicknamed "Vipers") from the 401st Tactical Fighter Wing (Provisional) share ramp space at Qatar's Doha International Airport with *Armée de l'Air* Dassault Mirage F-1C air defense fighters from the *12e Escadre de Chasse*. (DoD)

ATTACKER'S CAPABILITIES
The airpower of a global coalition

Desert Storm was, in effect, the NATO–Warsaw Pact war that never was, pitting largely Soviet weaponry, doctrine, and tactics against a Coalition, which reflected NATO strategic thinking. It was also a war that relied on broad international cooperation and coordination. Participation by non-American Coalition members was both widespread and essential. They provided all bases, airfields, and ports; over 90 percent of fuel; a third of all military personnel; a quarter of combat aircraft (and almost a third of all fighter and attack airplanes); nearly half of all naval ships and boats; and more than a third of all armour, mechanized artillery, and other vehicles. And they suffered for their efforts, taking a quarter of aircraft losses; over a third of combat deaths; and more than half of all wounded.

However, the United States furnished the bulk of military power. The US Air Force at this point had over 6,800 airplanes, including 2,798 fighter and attack aircraft, 366 strategic bombers, 555 air refueling tankers, and 824 airlifters, equipping 397 active duty and reserve squadrons. The Air Force Reserve and the Air Guard added another 2,200 aircraft, bringing the combined active force, Air Reserve, and Air Guard total to 9,032 aircraft, these being flown, maintained, and supported by nearly 528,000 active duty and over 500,000 Reserve, Guard, and other personnel. The US Navy, likewise at the pinnacle of its Cold War strength, had 14 carrier battle groups with each affiliated air wing deploying roughly 80 aircraft; 16 aircraft carriers; 4 battleships; 43 cruisers; 68 destroyers; 100 frigates; 61 amphibious assault ships; 99 submarines; and over 4,000 sea-and-land-based operational aircraft, of which nearly 2,700 were coded as "fleet combat" for air defense, attack, antisubmarine, maritime patrol, and electronic intelligence and electronic warfare. Manning these ships, aircraft, and installations were over 570,000 active duty sailors, and another 430,000 Reserve and other personnel.

COALITION CONTRIBUTION BY GLOBAL ORIGIN					
Regional and national grouping[1]		Personnel[2]	Aircraft[3]	Vessels[4]	Vehicles[5]
The Americas	United States, Canada, Argentina, and Honduras	543,206	2,032	150	3,880
Africa, Middle East, South Asia, and Southwest Asia	Afghanistan, Bahrain, Bangladesh, Egypt, Free Kuwait, Morocco, Niger, Oman, Pakistan, Qatar, Saudi Arabia, Senegal, Sierra Leone, Syria, Turkey, UAE	168,551	466	34	1,549
Europe	Belgium, Czechoslovakia, Denmark, France, Germany, Greece, Hungary, Italy, Netherlands, Norway, Poland, Portugal, Romania, Spain, Sweden, Turkey, UK	66,898	155	70	888
Oceania and East/Southeast Asia	Australia, New Zealand, Philippines, Singapore, South Korea, Japan[6]	2,068	7	3	2,000
Total		780,723	2,660	257	8,317

[1]Not every country contributed in every category.
[2]Includes soldiers, sailors, airmen, Marines/other naval uniformed personnel, and medical personnel (including chemical/biological warfare teams).
[3]Includes fighters, bombers, attack/strike aircraft, combat transports, special operations aircraft, but not approximately 2,000 Coalition helicopters assigned to land forces (approximately 1,700 of which were US), which were not controlled by the Joint Force Air Component Commander (JFACC).
[4]Includes all large naval combatants and their support vessels, as well as submarines, missile boats, gun boats, and other patrol craft.
[5]Includes main battle tanks (MBTs), armoured personnel carriers (APCs), tank destroyers, scout and armoured cars, self-propelled guns and rocket batteries, and other combat support vehicles, but not towed artillery.
[6]Japan furnished the 2,000 vehicles listed, all of which were light utility and personnel vans.

The US-led Central Command (USCENTCOM), under the command of US Army Gen H. Norman Schwarzkopf (the "CINCCENT") and the Saudi Arabian-led Joint Forces Command (JFC), under the command of Saudi air defense command Lt Gen Khaled bin Sultan bin Abd-al-Aziz divided between them the command and control of Coalition forces. CENTCOM and the JFC were co-equal and interdependent, with both acting in coordination via a Coalition Coordination Communications and Integration Center (C³IC). While Khaled, trained in British and American military academies and war colleges and thus broadly experienced with both the British and American military services and systems, recognized it was "inevitable that the command structure of the air campaign should reflect American supremacy," he also "wanted to be sure that [he] knew 100 percent of what was going on." Schwarzkopf understood this, noting that from their first meeting, he and Khaled "became true friends and effective colleagues."

American forces, assigned to CENTCOM (over which Gen Schwarzkopf exercised operational control or "OPCON") were divided into four service-specific subordinate commands:

Central Command Air Forces (CENTAF), commanded by Lt Gen Charles "Chuck" Horner USAF;

Army forces Central Command (ARCENT), under Lt Gen John Yeosock USA;

Naval forces Central Command (NAVCENT), under VADM Stanley "Stan" Arthur USN; and

Marine forces Central Command (MARCENT), under Lt Gen Walter "Walt" Boomer USMC.

Central Command's Special Operations Forces (SOF) came under a subordinate joint command, SOCCENT, headed by Col Jesse Johnson USA.

Other Coalition forces were split between CENTCOM and the JFC, with France under the JFC during *Desert Shield*, and under CENTCOM during *Desert Storm*.

Lieutenant General Charles "Chuck" Horner, the Joint and Combined Force Air Component Commander, oversaw the planning and execution of the *Desert Storm* air campaign. A veteran USAF fighter pilot and fighter commander, he was determined not to repeat the mistakes of Vietnam's infamous *Rolling Thunder* campaign. (DoD)

Each of the "-CENT" commanders wore multiple hats. Gen Schwarzkopf, as "CINCCENT," exerted operational control over the airmen of both CENTAF and NAVCENT, and, as well, had designated himself the joint force land component commander, which, because he had operational control over ARCENT and MARCENT, meant that Schwarzkopf effectively had operational control over their aviation elements as well.

Lt Gen Horner, a veteran fighter pilot with extensive combat and leadership experience, commanded CENTAF, and, most significantly, served as Schwarzkopf's joint force air component commander (JFACC), making him the single most important figure in the history of the air war in *Desert Storm*. As JFACC, Horner exercised tactical control over the Coalition partners' aircraft, though they remained under the command of their nations' militaries. No jingoistic war-lover, Horner was a man of quiet but strong personal faith with a great reverence for life, not only of those soldiers, sailors, airmen, and Marines in the Coalition, and their allies, but also of the enemy. That same faith, coupled with Midwestern practicality and common-sense, played well with the other Coalition leaders, many of whom became close friends.

VADM Arthur, commander of the Seventh Fleet and NAVCENT served as joint force naval component commander, which included two carrier battle forces – Battle Force Zulu (Task Force 154) and Battle Force Yankee (Task Force 155) – and shore-based naval aviation.

Lt Gen Boomer commanded both MARCENT and the First Marine Expeditionary Force (I MEF).

While the Coalition nations and services exercised *command* over their aircraft and airmen, Horner exercised *tactical control* (TACON) over them, coordinating with CENTCOM and the JFC. As Schwarzkopf put it to chief air planner Brig Gen Buster Glosson, "If you aren't part of the air campaign under Horner, you don't fly," and he made the policy stick.

As CENTCOM Forward in the opening weeks of the crisis, Horner had responsibility to oversee the bedding down of arriving Coalition forces across the Gulf region. For air power forces the problem was particularly acute. Working with the Saudis, Horner pragmatically established four "composite" provisional air divisions to concentrate all Air Force aircraft deployed to CENTCOM's area of responsibility (AOR) according to their function.

Easing the rapid move of defensive forces to the Gulf was Saudi Arabia's massive investment in military infrastructure. Over the 1980s, the Saudis had built a number of facilities, bases, and cantonments, including four huge "Military Cities" named after Kings Abd al-Aziz (Tabuk), Fahd (Dhahran), Faisal (Khamis Mushait), and Khaled (Hafr al-Batin). These included a port on the Persian Gulf at Ras al Mishab, as well as an air logistics center (ALC) equivalent in capabilities to any American ALC. Additionally, Saudi workers had built numerous civil airfields to support the *Hadj*, the massive religious pilgrimage made to Mecca, Islam's holiest site. These were all invaluable in responding to Iraq. To give two examples, Dhahran eventually received half of all strategic airlift missions during *Desert Shield* and *Desert Storm*; Jeddah, gateway to Mecca, hosted B-52G bombers and KC-135 and KC-10 tankers, which shared ramp space with Saudi C-130Hs.

One payoff came from CENTCOM having previously established munitions stockpiles in Oman at Thumrait, Seeb, and Masirah, and at Diego Garcia, pre-positioning three munitions-loaded ships as well. Thus, when Iraq invaded Kuwait, it had 48,000 short tons of munitions on hand including nearly 42,000 Mk-82 500lb bombs, over 7,000 Mk-84 2,000lb bombs, 12,090 Mk-117 750lb bombs; 500 2,000lb GBU-10 laser-guided bombs (LGBs); 630 500lb GBU-12 LGBs; over 3 million 20mm rounds; 600,000 30mm rounds, and

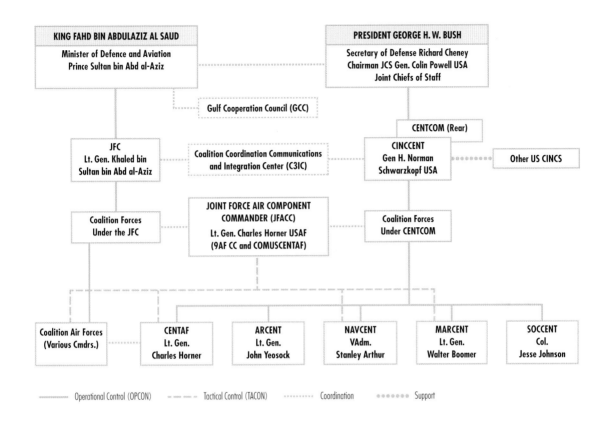

ABOVE COALITION CHAIN OF COMMAND

USAF Provisional Air Divisions

The 14th Air Division (Provisional) under Brig Gen Buster Glosson (also serving as Horner's head of campaign plans) contained nearly 750 fighters, battlefield attack, and electronic warfare jamming aircraft.

The 15th Air Division (Provisional) under Brig Gen Glenn A. Profitt II (who succeeded Brig Gen Larry "Poobah" Henry, who had planned the suppression of enemy air defenses (SEAD) campaign before leaving for another assignment), with nearly 90 aircraft, covered Wild Weasel "kinetic" suppression of enemy air defenses (SEAD), tactical reconnaissance, airborne early warning, and battle management.

The 16th Air Division (Provisional) under Brig Gen Edwin E. Tenoso – also known as the *16th Airlift Division (Provisional)* – had nearly 160 aircraft covering all tactical and executive airlift, and medical evacuation.

The 17th Air Division (Provisional) under Brig Gen Patrick P. Caruana, concentrated air refueling, strategic reconnaissance and communications, and some of the 96 B-52 strategic bombers employed in the war, totaling just under 400 aircraft.

As well as these four Air Divisions, Horner had tactical control over US–European Command's Joint Task Force *Proven Force* (technically the 7440th Composite Wing (Provisional), under Maj Gen James L. Jamerson, with another 160 aircraft.

Proven Force, operating out of Incirlik Air Base (outside Adana, Turkey) was a self-contained air expeditionary force (to use a later term) comprised of fighters, strike aircraft, Wild Weasel, jamming, airborne early warning, tankers, electronic intelligence collectors, and special operations forces. Echoing early Cold War composite air strike forces and even the first air commandos of World War II, it became a harbinger of the Air Force's Air Expeditionary Forces deployed routinely to the Middle East from the mid-1990s onwards.

RSAF Lockheed C-130H Hercules tactical transports ("Herks") from No. 4 Squadron share ramp space with deployed Boeing B-52G Stratofortresses ("Buffs") from the 1708th Bomb Wing (P) at Jeddah's King Abdulaziz International Airport, better known as the aerial gateway to Mecca. Jeddah Buffs flew over half of all B-52G Gulf War strikes. (DoD)

other munitions; all of which, when inspected, were found to be "combat-ready." "When," as Horner recalled, "our aircraft landed at Gulf airfields they were met with spares, fuel, munitions, living facilities, and all the other things they would need to survive and fight. This materiel had been stored on ships anchored in theatre and in leased warehouses throughout the AOR [Area of Responsibility]."

COALITION FIXED WING AIRCRAFT BY NATION AND MISSION AREA					
Nation	Fighter/Attack	Tanker	Airlift	Other	Total
United States	1,323	285	175	207	1,990
Saudi Arabia	276	15	38	10	339
United Kingdom	57	9	3	8	77
France	44	3	12	7	66
Kuwait	40	–	3	–	43
Oman	~20	–	–	–	~20
Canada	24	1	12	2	39
Bahrain	24	–	–	–	24
Qatar	20	–	–	–	20
United Arab Emirates	20	–	–	–	20
Italy	8	–	3	1	12
South Korea	–	–	5	–	5
New Zealand	–	–	2	–	2
Argentina	–	–	3	–	3
Total by mission area	1,856	313	256	235	2,660
Figures vary widely among sources; the author has chosen what in his view are the most accurate or plausible.					

OPPOSITE
Grumman's EA-6B Prowler was one of the war's essential airplanes, critical for jamming Iraqi air defense radars, undertaking other jamming and electronic combat missions, and supporting both airborne strike and surface operations. A derivative of the early-1960s A-6A Intruder all-weather attack bomber, it had a four-person crew. Here one from VAQ-136 is shown immediately after trapping aboard the USS *Kitty Hawk* (CV-63). (DoD)

Of the Coalition's 2,660 combat and combat-support fixed-wing aircraft, 2,203 were based at more than two dozen civil airports and military airfields across Saudi Arabia, the United Arab Emirates, Bahrain, Oman, Qatar, and Turkey. The remaining 457 were deployed on six carriers in the Persian Gulf, Gulf of Oman, and the Red Sea.

Not counted among these were aircraft such as B-52 bombers, KC-135 and KC-10 tankers, and C-141 and C-5 airlifters based in the United States ("CONUS"), Europe, Egypt, and Diego Garcia. As well, this does not include approximately 2,000 Coalition helicopters and fixed-wing organic army and Marine aviation assets which furnished troop lift, scout, aerial fire support, and other missions for their commanding land forces, and which did not come under the tasking or tactical control of the Coalition's JFACC.

By mission area, 1,856 of these 2,660 were air superiority, strike fighter, SAM-suppression, and attack aircraft; 313 were tankers; and 256 were airlifters. Another 235 constituted a mix of strategic and tactical reconnaissance aircraft; electronic intelligence collectors; SOF gunships, air refuelers, airlifters, and helicopters for insertion and combat

search-and-rescue (CSAR); forward air controllers and air observation platforms; maritime patrol airplanes; battle management, command and control, and special tasking systems; psyops aircraft, communications jammers; and liaison aircraft.

The United States contributed 75 percent of all in-theater aircraft ashore and afloat. The numbers were staggering, including 115 A-6E Intruder attack bombers; 24 A-7E Corsair II light attack aircraft; 144 A-10A Thunderbolt II tank-busters; eight AC-130A/H Spectre gunships; 82 AV-8B Harrier II V/STOL fighter-bombers; 96 B-52G strategic bombers; 60 F-4G Wild Weasels; 100 F-14A/A+ Tomcat fleet air defense fighters; 174 McDonnell-Douglas F-15C/D Eagle and F-15E Strike Eagle air superiority and strike fighters; 363 F-16A/B/C/D Fighting Falcon fighter-bombers; 169 F/A-18A/C/D Hornet strike fighters; 38 EA-6B Prowler and 24 EF-111A Raven or "Sparkvark" electronic warfare aircraft, 88 F-111E/F Aardvark strike aircraft; and 42 F-117A Nighthawk "stealth" attack airplanes.

Electronic warfare aircraft and SAM-killers – particularly the EA-6B, EF-111, and the F-4G Wild Weasel – would play a vital role protecting strike packages in high-threat areas, as would airborne intelligence and jamming platforms such as the Boeing RC-135 Rivet Joint and Lockheed EC-130H Compass Call.

Battlefield and battlespace control systems such as the E-2 and E-3 AWACS, the EC-130 ABCCC, and the experimental E-8 J-STARS were essential for both detecting and tracking Iraqi forces, and preventing "blue-on-blue" friendly fire. The coalition's aerial tankers not only established the "Tanker Bridge" linking the Gulf region to America and Europe, but also

supported in-theater training, operations, and, of course, the air war. Aerial tanking represented an Anglo-American accomplishment over a half-century in the making, and, fittingly, among the dozen different tanker types flown in *Desert Shield–Desert Storm*, was the iconic KC-135, the first (and greatest) of all jet tanker-transports.

Next was Saudi Arabia, then the United Kingdom, France, and doughty little Kuwait, which between them furnished 20 percent of Coalition air strength, and the remaining Coalition partners contributed a further 5 percent. The combat forces and systems these fielded covered all aspects of air warfare: air superiority; fleet air defense; deep strike; battlefield air

Aerial tanking was essential to the air campaign against Iraq, and the Coalition deployed 13 different tanker designs to the Gulf, some with boom-dispensing systems but most with drogue and hose ones. Here is a Boeing KC-135E Stratotanker using water-injection on takeoff to support a Desert Storm mission. Of the 13 tanker types, the KC-135A/E/R family and its derivatives (the French KC-135F, Saudi KE-3A, and Canadian CC-137) were the most numerous. (DoD)

Air Force McDonnell-Douglas F-4G Wild Weasels with AGM-88 HARM, and, more rarely, older Vietnam era AGM-45 Shrike missiles destroyed many Iraqi SAM radars, intimidating operators into shutting down their equipment lest they be killed. The USAF deployed 60 F-4Gs to the Gulf, teams of "Weasel Police" covering strike packages through to the end of the war. (DoD)

operations (including air interdiction, close air support, aerial fire support, and troop lift); intelligence, surveillance, and reconnaissance; air-refueling; strategic and tactical air mobility; and space-based intelligence, warning, weather, navigation, and communications.

On August 7, Operation *Desert Shield* began to deter, and if necessary, defend Saudi Arabia and the Gulf region from further Iraqi aggression. That day, the first American aircraft – 23 F-15C Eagles – left for the Gulf, and Prime Minister Margaret Thatcher ordered the RAF to send strike aircraft as well. The F-15Cs arrived on August 8, the same day that Tom King, the UK's Secretary of State for Defense, announced that British forces were prepared to deploy to the Gulf. On August 10, Marshal of the Royal Air Force Sir David Craig, then Chief of the Defence Staff, appointed ACM Sir Patrick "Paddy" Hine commander of British forces, headquartered at RAF High Wycombe. In turn, the next day Hine appointed AVM Ronald A.F. "Sandy" Wilson as Commander British Forces Arabian Peninsula (BFPA) headquartered in Riyadh.

Subsequently, at the beginning of October, BFPA became British Forces Middle East (BFME), and Hine appointed Lt Gen Sir Peter de la Billière, a distinguished SAS officer, as British theater commander, Wilson serving as his deputy and as air commander, essentially the same relationship Schwarzkopf had with Horner. Still further, on November 17, 1990, Wilson was succeeded by AVM William J. "Bill" Wratton, who took the RAF through the war, and worked extremely effectively with Chuck Horner.

The first British aircraft of what was now known as Operation *Granby* – a mix of 24 Tornado F.3 air defense fighters and 12 Jaguar GR.1A strike fighters – arrived in Dhahran and Thumrait, respectively, on August 11, and flew their first operational missions just two hours after arrival. (Tornado GR.1 strike aircraft deployed on August 27, following the resolution of a mini-debate within Whitehall over whether the RAF should deploy "offensive" or "defensive" aircraft.) VC10K tankers and Nimrod MR.2P maritime patrol planes flew to Thumrait and Seeb, respectively, and by mid-August the RAF was already well established in operational tempo. Over the next six weeks, the American and British combat aircraft arriving in the Gulf were joined by others from France, Italy, and Canada.

The first of over 60 French aircraft and helicopters, four Mirage F-1CR reconnaissance strike fighters, and four Mirage 2000 air defense fighters, arrived at Al Ahsa, Saudi Arabia on October 3, the beginning of Operation *Daguet*. The first Jaguar A strike fighters arrived a week later; France also sent eight Mirage F-1C air defense fighters to Doha. On September 25, eight Tornado IDS strike aircraft from Italy's Aeronautica Militare Italiana (AMI, the Italian Air Force), left Gioia del Colle for Al Dhafra. Finally, the first Canadian CF-18 Hornets arrived at Doha on October 7, assigned to fleet air defense duties over the northern and central Persian Gulf.

For their size, the other Coalition nations contributed significant strike capabilities, particularly: Saudi Arabia with its fleet of F-15C Eagles, Tornado ADV fighters and IDS strike aircraft, F/RF-5Es, and Hawk Mk 65; Canada with its CF-18 Hornets; Britain with the Nimrod MR.2P and R.1 maritime patrol and intelligence collection aircraft, and the Tornado F.3 and GR.1/1A, Jaguar GR.1A, and Buccaneer S.2B strike aircraft (sent in mid-war to assist the Tornado force); France with their Mirage F-1, Mirage 2000, and Jaguar A fighter force; Qatar and the UAE with the Alpha Jet E, Mirage F-1, Mirage 2000; and Italy, flying the Tornado IDS. Kuwait had extracted a mix of A-4KUs, Mirage F-1CKs, and Hawk Mk 64 aircraft in a fighting withdrawal at once both remarkable and heroic, and now stood ready to fly them again, with "FREE KUWAIT" emblazoned on their camouflaged flanks.

Therefore, while the American contribution was the largest and most robust, the other Coalition members nevertheless provided a quarter of all fixed-wing aircraft, almost a third of all fighter and attack aircraft, and almost a third of all airlifters. *Desert Storm*, when it opened, was thus truly a coalition air war, and in more than just its diverse personnel.

Ordnance

Weapons – bombs both "smart" and "dumb," rockets, and guided missiles – gave the Coalition's strike aircraft a formidable punch. Though well over 90 percent of the Coalition's bombs and rockets were unguided, it possessed (for the time) impressive precision missiles and bombs that, at their most accurate, could strike a target within 10ft of a "Desired Mean Point of Impact" (DMPI, pronounced "Dimpy"). These reflected the American and European investment in precision "smart" weapons and airborne sensor technology over the 1970s and 1980s. While the vast majority of air weapons were American, the Coalition also brought special weapon capabilities unavailable to US forces – most notably the French AS-30L laser-guided missile (which Iraq employed as well), the British ALARM anti-radar missile and JP233 runway denial munition, and the Canadian CRV-7, the latter an unguided but extremely accurate podded rocket – that greatly enhanced strike and land-sea support operations.

"Smart" weapons had an impact out of all proportion to their numbers, for they enabled commanders and planners to think in terms of "nodal" warfare, of targets destroyed per sortie, not sorties required to destroy a single target. The result was simultaneous and parallel warfare – i.e. multiple aircraft going simultaneously to strike at dozens of aimpoints, and thus not the linear and sequential air attacks of previous wars where large formations struck at a single aimpoint, as with raids in World War II, or the anti-bridge campaigns in Korea and Vietnam. "Of the 85,000 tons of bombs used in the Gulf War, only 8,000 tons – less than ten percent – were PGMs," CENTAF's Director for Campaign Plans Brig Gen Buster C. Glosson noted after the war, "yet they accounted for nearly 75 percent of the damage."

The Coalition's international composition is evident from this flight of Qatari, French, US, and Canadian strike aircraft. Leading is a Qatari Emiri Air Force (QEAF) Dassault Mirage F-1EDA of No. 7 Air Superiority Squadron, flanked by an Armée de l'Air Dassault Mirage F-1C of the 12e Escadre de Chasse, and a USAF General Dynamics F-16C of the 401st TFW (P), 614th TFS. On the F-1C's wing is a Canadian Air Command CF-188 [CF-18] of the Desert Cats (an amalgam of 416 and 439 Squadrons); and a QEAF Dassault Alpha Jet E of the 11th Close Support Squadron flies on the wing of the F-16C. (DoD)

Training

COALITION PRINCIPAL GUIDED AIR WEAPONS				
Air-to-air missiles				
Weapon	Speed	Range	Guidance	Warhead
Raytheon AIM-7M Sparrow	M=3.5+	25 miles+	radar homing	90lb blast-fragmentation
Raytheon AIM-9L/M Sidewinder	M=2.8+	10 miles	infrared homing	21lb blast-fragmentation
Hughes AIM-54C Phoenix[1]	M=4.5+	100 miles+	radar homing	135lb blast-fragmentation
Hughes AIM-120A AMRAAM[2]	M=4.5	25 miles+	radar homing	45lb blast-fragmentation
BAe Dynamics Skyflash 90[1]	M=3.5+	28 miles	radar homing	90lb blast-fragmentation
Matra Super 530D/530F[1,3]	M=4/4.5	16–25 miles	radar homing	66lb blast-fragmentation
Matra R.550 Magic II[1,3]	M=3.5	20 miles	infrared homing	28lb blast-fragmentation

Air-, surface-, and sub-surface-launched cruise missiles				
Weapon	Speed	Range	Guidance	Warhead
Boeing AGM-86C CALCM	M=0.75	750 miles+	INS/GPS[4]	blast initiated dispenser[5]
Gen Dyn BGM-109 TLAM-C[6]	M=0.75	750 miles+	INS/radar/TM[7]	1,000lb blast-fragmentation
Gen Dyn BGM-109 TLAM-D[6]	M=0.75	750 miles+	INS/radar/TM[7]	166 BLU-97/B bomblets
Guided air-to-surface missiles				
Weapon	Speed	Range	Guidance	Warhead
Aérospatiale AS-30L3	M=1.4	6 miles+	laser	528lb SAP HE penetrator
Martin Mar. AGM-62B Walleye II	M=0.9	25 miles+	electro-optical	2,015lb shaped charge
Hughes AGM-65B/D/Maverick	M=0.9	17 miles+	electro-optical/IIR[8]	125lb HEAT shaped charge
Hughes AGM-65E/G Maverick	M=0.9	17 miles	laser/IIR	300lb HE penetrator
McD-D AGM-84E SLAM[9]	M=0.7	70 miles+	electro-opt/GPS/IIR[10]	488lb blast-fragmentation
Texas Instruments AGM-45 Shrike	M=1.5+	25 miles	radar homing	149lb blast-fragmentation
Raytheon AGM-88B HARM[11]	M=1.5+	30 miles+	radar homing	144lb blast-fragmentation
BAe Dynamics ALARM[12]	M=2.0	60 miles	INS/radar homing	HE blast-fragmentation[13]
Hughes BGM-71D/E TOW 2/2A[14]	M=0.9	2.33 miles	wire guided	13lb HEAT shaped charge
Rockwell AGM-114A/B/C Hellfire	M=1.25	4 miles+	laser	20lb HEAT shaped charge
BAe Dynamics Sea Skua	M=0.8+	15 miles+	radar homing	62lb blast-fragmentation
EE AGM-123A Skipper II	M=0.9	15 miles+	laser	1,000lb mod Mk 83 bomb
Guided bombs					
Weapon	Weight	Guidance	Basic bomb	Aircraft using	Range[15]
GBU-10	2,000lb	Laser Paveway I/II	Mk 84, BLU-109	A-6E, F-15E, F-111F, F-117	2.8–7.5 miles
GBU-12	500lb	Laser Paveway II	Mk. 82	A-6E, F-15E, F-111F	2.8–7.5 miles
GBU-15	2,000lb	TV/Imaging IR[16]	Mk 84	F-111F	~15 miles
GBU-16	1,000lb	Laser Paveway II	Mk 83	A-6E	2.8–7.5 miles
GBU-24	2,000lb	Laser Paveway III	Mk 84, BLU-109	F-111F	2.8–18.5 miles
GBU-27	2,000lb	Laser Pave. III (mod.)	I-2,000	F-117	2.8–18.5 miles
GBU-28	4,700lb	Laser Paveway III	Bespoke Design	F-111F	2.8–18.5 miles
UK-1000	1,000lb	Laser Paveway II	RAF Mk 13/18	UK Tornado GR.1	2.8–7.5 miles
BGL-400	1,036lb	Laser TMV-630 Eblis	FrAF BL-70	Fr Jaguar A	?–6.2 miles

[1] Not fired "in anger" during the war.

[2] Advanced medium range air-to-air missile; the first AIM-120As arrived very late in the war, and, while carried on USAF F-15Cs, were not launched against Iraqi aircraft.

[3] Iraqi F-1s also employed Super 530D, R.550, and AS-30L missiles.

[4] INS = Inertial Navigation System; GPS = Global Positioning System.

[5] Later CALCMS (Conventional Air-Launched Cruise Missiles) had 3,000lb blast-fragmentation warheads, but not those used in the Gulf War.

[6] TLAM = Tomahawk Land Attack Missile.

[7] TM = Terrain Matching via digitized image correlation.

[8] EO = electro-optical (AGM-65B); IIR = Imaging Infrared (AGM-65D).

[9] SLAM = Standoff Land Attack Missile.

[10] SLAM employed a data link, EO seeker video, GPS midcourse guidance, and terminal IIR guidance.

[11] HARM = High-Speed Anti-Radiation Missile.

[12] ALARM = Air-Launched Anti-Radiation Missile.

[13] Precise HE weight unknown.

[14] TOW = Tube Launched, Optically Tracked, Wire-Guided.

[15] Depending upon launch altitude, speed, and attitude at release.

[16] GBU-15(V)1/B employed TV guidance and GBU-15(V)2/B used Imaging Infrared (IIR).

At least as significant as the aircraft and weapons was the quality of the force. Following disasters and disappointments in Vietnam, Desert One, Grenada, and Lebanon, the services embarked on more intensive and realistic training programs, establishing instrumented ranges to assess student and unit performance. The Navy's Top Gun program at Miramar NAS; "Strike University" at Fallon's Naval Strike Warfare Center; the Marine Corps' air-ground training program at Yuma MCAS; and the Air Force's Fighter Weapons School and Red Flag team-building strike package training at Nellis AFB, gave American combat aircrews the skills to survive and emerge victorious from their first encounters with enemy airmen and air defenders, rather than simply throwing them into the "deep end" and leaving them to fend for themselves as had happened in Vietnam at the time of Operation *Rolling Thunder*. Flying agile, small (and thus difficult-to-see) aircraft such as the Douglas A-4F Skyhawk and Northrop F-5E Tiger II, aggressor pilots emulated Soviet tactics, and the training ranges had emitters and even faux SAMs emulating radar-and-SAM intensive threat environments.

Top Gun Douglas A-4F Skyhawk (Bu No. 155000), flown by Lt Dave "Shooter" Vanderschoot, photographed on the Nellis AFB, Nevada ramp by LCDR Dave Parsons during an exchange visit by the Naval Fighter Weapons School at Miramar NAS, California to the USAF's Fighter Weapons School. (DoD)

Air Force Tactical Air Command's then-secret Constant Peg program enabled selected Air Force, Navy, and Marine fighter pilots to fly against actual MiG-17, MiG-21, and MiG-23 fighters. A select band of tactics instructors drawn from the Air Force, Navy, and Marines taught airmen the strengths and weaknesses of these commonly found threats, and, perhaps most importantly, removed the often seconds-robbing mystique and allure that they possessed. "The first time I saw a MiG, I was so fascinated I momentarily stared, and that's fatal in combat," said one Constant Peg veteran; "After that, it was just 'There's a MiG, fight's on.'"

The Air Force's Red Flags spawned other training exercises, including Green Flag (for electronic combat), Blue Flag (for command and control), Maple Flag (in Canada), and Cope Thunder (in the Philippines). NATO and other allied airmen, invited to participate in these exercises, imparted the lessons learned to their own forces. A quarter-century after *Desert Storm*, Royal Air Force Air Chief Marshal Sir William "Bill" Wratten RAF recalled "All of the US forces and many of the Coalition air forces had been through the Flag programmes. We all spoke the same language. We knew the terminology. We were accustomed to force package thinking, and that is why it glued together remarkably well and extremely quickly."

USAF airmen inspect an Egyptian Air Force Mikoyan MiG-19S (NATO Farmer-C) fighter during Exercise *Bright Star 83*. (DoD)

International programs such as the NATO Tiger Meets (held since 1961), the NATO Reforger exercises in Germany, and the Bright Star exercises in Egypt further honed readiness and interoperability, forging bonds among American, NATO, and Middle Eastern military leaders, and giving all participants a set of shared familiarity, experiences, and insights that proved invaluable to planners and operators as they confronted Saddam Hussein.

In sum, then, as 1990 drew to a close, Coalition leaders were confident they had the force, the aircraft, the weapons, and the people to get the job done if war came.

DEFENDER'S CAPABILITIES
Iraq's military machine

The invading armed forces

As the region's most powerful military power, Iraq posed a formidable threat to other Gulf nations, particularly Saudi Arabia, its vast southern oil-rich neighbor. In August 1990, its military outnumbered Saudi Arabia's in manpower by 15 to 1; in aircraft by almost 4 to 1; in tanks by more than 10 to 1; in other mechanized vehicles by nearly 5 to 1; and in artillery by almost 8 to 1.

Particularly worrying was the Saddam regime's laser-focus on chemical and biological weapons (and its demonstrated willingness to use them, both against Iran and its own people, a single attack at Halabja killing between 3,000 to 7,000 Kurds), and atomic weaponry as well. Of particular concern – again because so little was then known, aside from their widespread use in the Iran–Iraq War – were Iraq's ballistic missiles, maintained by the Surface-to-Surface Missiles Directorate (SSMD), commanded by Lt Gen Hazem Abd al Razzaq al Ayyubi, and naval coastal defense antishipping missiles, overseen by Iraqi Navy Colonel [sic] Muzahim Mustafa. The former threatened Iraq's neighbors and, more distantly, Israel; the latter threatened naval forces that might approach through the Persian Gulf.

Iraq had entered the ballistic missile age in 1974 when, looking to strike at Israel, it contracted with the Soviet Union for the first of what would eventually total 819 Soviet R-17 (NATO SS-1C Scud-B) ballistic missiles, together with 11 eight-wheel self-propelled MAZ-543 (9P117 Uragan) transporter-erector-launchers (TELs). Ironically, their first use was to the east, against Iran. During the Iran–Iraq War, Hussein's missileers launched over 200 Scuds against Iran, but while Iran could strike Baghdad with its own Scuds, Iraq could not reach the Iranian capital of Teheran, as the Scud-B only possessed a 300km (187 miles) range.

This impelled the Hussein regime to begin a program – assisted by foreign equipment purchases – to increase the range of its missile force. The result was the Al-Hussein, with a smaller warhead – just 500kg (1,100lb) vice 1,000kg (2,200lb) – enabling a doubling of range so that it could now reach Teheran. Still not content, Iraqi engineers next developed a

900km (560-mile) stretched Scud derivative, the Al Abbas, though it proved a failure. They next started ambitious programs for even longer-range missiles and launch vehicles for space access, though none of the latter reached fruition either before or after the first Gulf War.

By the time of the Gulf War, Iraq possessed approximately 600 Scud- and Scud-derivative Al-Hussein missiles (intelligence estimates at the time ranged from 350 to 950), including 25 with botulinum, anthrax, and aflatoxin warheads (though not known at the time), operated by two missile brigades. It had five missile complexes and 28 fixed launchers clustered around H-1, H-2, and H-3 airfields in western Iraq, and approximately 30 mobile launchers consisting of the Soviet-origin MAZ-543 TEL, and the Al-Waleed, an indigenous mobile erector-launcher (MEL) derived from the commercial Saab-Scania tractor-trailer.

The SSMD operated a brigade of the 70km (43.5-mile) Soviet 9M21 (NATO FROG-7, FROG = "Free Rocket Over Ground") and a 90km (56-mile) Iraqi derivative, the Laith, also TEL-launched. Here is a FROG-7 on the launch rail of its ZIL-135 TEL, captured after the 2003 invasion. (DoD)

Control of the Al-Hussein force was via encrypted communications over land-lines, making "left of launch" deployment and firing preparation virtually impossible to detect. The scope, structure, command and control, and operational construct of Iraq's missile forces was neither well understood nor fully appreciated until after the war; as the GWAPS concluded (v. 4, p. 282), "Postwar intelligence suggests that the estimated number of missiles was somewhat high, the estimated number of TELs and MELs was somewhat low, and predictions of tactics and organizational structure were inaccurate."

The tiny Iraqi Navy, home-ported at Umm Qasr, nevertheless posed a surprisingly significant threat, through mine warfare and antishipping missiles. Its missile inventory

Iraqi military strength, 1990

Overall, at the onset of the Gulf crisis, Iraq possessed approximately:

950,000 soldiers in 60 divisions (42 along its southern and south-eastern border), and an estimated 850,000 reservists, all ostensibly hardened by over nearly a decade of war against neighboring Iran

4,900 tanks of Soviet and Chinese origin, 3,500 towed and mobile artillery pieces, and 7,500 other mechanized vehicles

165 naval craft (including 13 with Soviet Styx and French Exocet antishipping missiles), mine warfare vessels, patrol boats, and amphibious craft

50 Silkworm anti-ship missiles (a Chinese variant of the Soviet Styx) deployed in seven coastal defense installations

600 Scud and Scud-derivative Al-Hussein ballistic missiles, with approximately 30 transporter-erector-launchers (TELs) and 28 fixed launchers

Long-and short-range mobile battlefield rocket artillery systems

4,000 tons of mustard gas and nerve agents

Bio-agent shells, bombs, and rocket and missile warheads (this was suspected, but not known until after the war).

KARI, a sophisticated French-built integrated air defense system (IADS) blending Soviet and Western radars, communications, and missile systems

9,000 fixed and mobile antiaircraft artillery (AAA) cannon

Over 150 surface-to-air (SAM) sites, and 16,000 SAMs, consisting of 7,000 radar-guided Soviet, French, and US (the latter Raytheon I-HAWKS captured from Kuwait) missiles, and 9,000 infrared-seeking man-portable ones.

Over 950 Soviet, Chinese, French, and Italian airplanes and helicopters, including Soviet and French interceptors, fighters, bombers, and attack aircraft and 160 attack helicopters, operating from 24 airfields and 30 dispersal bases, armed with sophisticated air-to-air and guided air-to-surface missiles and bombs included the Soviet SS-N-2 Styx (Soviet P-15/20 Termit), its more numerous and capable Chinese derivative, the CSS-N-2 Silkworm (Chinese HY-2G Hai Ying), and the French AM-39 Exocet.

Altogether, at the onset of hostilities, Iraq possessed 13 missile boats of four different types, including six captured from Kuwait. As well, it fielded seven Silkworm launchers ashore, and approximately 50 Silkworm missiles housed in a Kuwait City school taken over for storage and assembly. Finally, the Iraqi Navy possessed seven Aérospatiale SA 321H Super Frelon helicopters, equipped with Omera ORB-31D search radars and the ability to launch Exocet antishipping missiles.

Saddam's air power

While Iraq's massive land forces, now perched on Kuwait's border with Saudi Arabia, constituted a clear danger to Saudi Arabia, its air forces and air defense forces commanded no less respect. Commanded by Lt Gen Muzahim Sa'b Hassan Al-Tikriti, in 1990 the Iraqi Air Force (IrAF) was both the largest of all Middle East air forces and a combat-proven air arm. It had a robust basing and support infrastructure, including 594 bunker-like aircraft shelters built by Belgian, British, French, and Yugoslavian contractors, many having concrete-and-steel blast doors weighing as much as 60 tons and hardened to withstand even the blast overpressures generated by a tactical nuclear weapon, distributed across 17 major airfields. The major airfields themselves were huge, larger even than an international airport like London Heathrow. "I had never seen anything like it before," recalled Soviet MiG-29 instructor Sergey Bezlyudnyy; "the equipment, shelters, and blast walls – everything was the last word in equipment and of outstanding quality."

In January 1991, the Iraqi Air Force had a reported 636 operational combat aircraft in 40 squadrons, consisting of 76 Dassault Mirage F-1EQ/BQ fighter-bombers; 33 MiG-29A Fulcrum fighters; 19 MiG-25PD/PDS Foxbat interceptors; nine recce MiG-25R; 38 MiG-23BN Flogger fighter-bombers; 68 MiG-23MK/ML/MS Flogger fighters; 174 MiG-21MF, MiG-21bis Fishbed (and its Chinese copy, the Chengdu F-7B Fishcan) fighters; 62 anti-armour Sukhoi Su-25K Frogfoots; 30 deep-strike Sukhoi Su-24MK Fencers; 114 Sukhoi Su-20/22 Fitter fighter-bombers; and three Tupolev Tu-16KSR-1-11 Badger strategic bombers (plus four of its Chinese derivative the Xian B-6D). In addition, there were over 300 armed trainers, transports, and other support aircraft, bringing the Iraqi Air Force's total to over 950 aircraft.

The Iraqi Air Force fielded 11 squadrons of the aging Mikoyan MiG-21 (NATO Fishbed) and a Chinese derivative, the Chengdu F-7B (Fishcan), totaling 174 aircraft that, altogether, accounted for a third of all Iraqi fighters. The most numerous variant was the MiG-21MF Fishbed-J, a Sudanese example of which is shown at an Egyptian base in 1983. The strengths and weaknesses of the MiG-21 were well known to Coalition airmen, the type having been thoroughly evaluated from the mid-1960s onwards. (DoD)

At 106 airplanes, the variable-sweep Mikoyan MiG-23ML and MiG-23BN (NATO Flogger) accounted for 20 percent of all Iraqi fighters. Like all Iraqi fighters, it was an aircraft the strengths and weaknesses of which were fully understood from detailed USAF evaluation and exploitation, as well as the post-1989 intelligence sweep of East German and other Warsaw Pact air forces. Wickedly fast and an extraordinary accelerator, the MiG-23 was a dangerously unforgiving airplane that demanded careful handling, particularly as it experienced markedly reduced lateral–directional stability at and above Mach 2. This MiG-23MS Flogger E was flown in the 4477th TES' Constant Peg joint service fighter familiarization program. (DoD)

Despite this, however, its structure and operating doctrine were strongly defensive and excessively centralized, inhibiting the ability of its airmen to undertake independent action outside a complex (if well-integrated) air defense system (IADS), which blended Soviet doctrine, a mix of Western and Communist-bloc electronic systems, a mishmash of French- and Soviet-origin combat aircraft, and a largely Soviet-origin missile force.

IRAQI AIR FORCE STRENGTH BY AIRCRAFT TYPE, FUNCTION, AND NUMBER OF SQUADRONS		
Aircraft type	Function	No. of squadrons
Dassault Mirage F-1EQ	air defense and surface attack	4
Mikoyan MiG-25PD/PDS/PU/RB Foxbat	air defense and reconnaissance	2
Mikoyan MiG-23BN Flogger-H	surface attack, secondary air defense	1
Mikoyan MiG-23ML Flogger-G	air defense	3
Mikoyan MiG-21MF Fishbed/Chengdu F-7B	air defense, secondary surface attack	4
Sukhoi Su-25K Frogfoot	battlefield air attack/antiarmour	2
Sukhoi Su-24MK Fencer	deep strike and surface attack	2
Sukhoi Su-22 Fitter	surface attack, secondary air defense	4
Sukhoi Su-20 Fitter	surface attack	1
Total		23

The Iraqi Air Force had 33 MiG-29A Fulcrums, at the time the Soviet Union's most advanced warplane. However, Iraqi airmen had low regard for it, despite its excellent agility, powerful twin engines, and good mix of sensors and weaponry. (DoD)

Further, many of its aircraft were well-worn after years of service against Iran, and thus the actual number of combat-ready and in-service aircraft was often quite lower than credited. On the eve of the war, Iraq had 20–25 serviceable Mirage F-1EQs, 25 serviceable MiG-29A Fulcrums (an aircraft for which Iraqi airmen had a surprisingly low regard despite its much-hyped alleged performance in the world's aviation press), and just 15 of the formidable MiG-25PD/PDS Foxbat. Of its 106 MiG-23 Floggers, only 30–35 MiG-23ML Flogger-Gs were fully combat capable. It could field 60 of the aging Vietnam-legacy MiG-21MF and its Chinese copy, the Chengdu F-7B. The 68

"bomb-truck" Su-22M Fitters were a reliable and rugged strike aircraft, equivalent, in many respects, to the Vietnam-era F-105. The 62 Su-25 Frogfoots, roughly equivalent to the American A-10, had done stellar service during the war with Iran and could be expected to do so again, if Iraq could gain at least parity in the struggle for air superiority over the battlespace, but were so hard-worn that only two squadrons were operational. Altogether, as revealed in a captured Iraqi dossier relating the findings of a "hot wash" postwar examination of the IrAF's performance, Iraq only had 23 fully combat-capable fighter and attack squadrons. Still, it was a dangerous force. Its obsolescing but plentiful MiG-21 force, the MiG-23MLs, MiG-25PD/PDS Foxbats, MiG-29As, and Dassault Mirage F-1EQs were armed with a mix of Soviet air-to-air radar-guided and heat-seeking (infrared) missiles (in many cases, sometimes the same missile, in two variations, one radar and one IR).

Contemplating the likely form Coalition attacks would take – the Iraqi high command appreciated that attacks would come from the south, southwest, northwest, and north, and along the coast, but would likely avoid Kuwait, at least at first – the IrAF determined to increase its available interceptor force by arming training variants of the MiG-21. It was confident it could confront adversaries attacking the Iraqi heartland, and hoped to negate some of the Coalition's advantages by intercepting AWACS aircraft, TR-1 reconnaissance aircraft, and even Coalition aircraft on their return to base.

Organization

The IrAF, and Air Defense Forces (IrADF, the latter headquartered at Rashid Air Base outside Baghdad and commanded by Maj Gen Shahin Yassin Muhammad) exercised shared responsibility for air defense. An Air Defense Operations Center (ADOC) at Muthenna AB established engagement priorities, using a French-developed computerized Command and Control (C2) system known as KARI ("Iraq" in French spelled backwards), and linked to other elements in the air defense system by buried fiber-optic cables and microwave (line-of-sight or tropo-scatter) relay towers.

Iraq's air defenders divided the country into four Air Defense Sectors (ADS) covering, respectively, North, South, West, and Central-East. Each ADS possessed a Sector Operations Center; several subordinate Intercept Operations Centers (IOC); at least one surface-to-air missile (SAM) brigade averaging 12 missile batteries; and at least two warning and control regiments that fed warnings from radar sites and observation posts to each IOC.

Iraq possessed nearly 500 early-warning radars and hundreds of acquisition and fire control ones associated with surface-to-air missile and antiaircraft systems. Altogether, this diverse assortment of radar systems – totaling over two dozen, most Soviet but with also some French systems – furnished coverage from low altitude through the mid-stratosphere, and into neighboring countries as well.

IRAQI AIR DEFENSE RADARS			
Radar (NATO name)	Range (miles/km)	Frequency	Purpose
SKB P-8 Volga (Knife Rest A)	155 miles/250km	A band (VHF)	EW/GCI[1]
SKB P-10 Volga A (Knife Rest B)	155miles/250km	A band (VHF)	EW/GCI
SKB P-12 Yenisei (Spoon Rest B/C)	115miles/185km	A band (VHF)	EW/acquisition
SKB P-14 Len (Tall King A/B/C)	250 miles/400km	A band (VHF)	EW/acquisition
VNIIRT P-15 Trail (Flat Face A)	140 miles/230km	C band (UHF)	EW/acquisition
VNIIRT P-15M Trail (Squat Eye)	140 miles/230km	C band (UHF)	EW/acquisition
VNIIRT P-19 Danube (Flat Face B)	160 miles/260km	C band (UHF)	EW/acquisition
NIIDAR P-35M/P-37 Saturn (Bar Lock)	140 miles/230km	E/F band	EW/GCI
NIIP P-40 Bronya (Long Track)	230 miles/370km	C band (UHF)	EW/acquisition
Thomson-CSF TRS-2105 Tiger G[2]	70 miles/113km	G band	EW/acquisition
Thomson-CSF TRS-2100 Tiger-S	70 miles/113km	S band	EW/acquisition
PRV-9 (Thin Skin)	150 miles/240km	H band	height-finder
PRV-11 (Side Net)	110 miles/176km	E band	height-finder
Thomson-CSF TRS-2205	335 miles/540km	E/F band	height-finder
Thomson CSF TRS-2215	335 miles/540km	E/F band	height-finder
Thomson CSF TRS-2230	335 miles/540km	E/F band	height-finder
Area and point-defense "partnered" fire control radars			
Radar (NATO name)	Range (miles/km)	Purpose	
SON-9 (Fire Can)	22 miles/35km	used to direct 57mm and 100mm AAA	
SON-30 (Fire Wheel)	22 miles/35km	paired with EW radars, used to direct 130mm AAA	
SON-50 (Flap Wheel)	22 miles/35km	used to direct 57mm AAA	
SNR-75 (Fan Song B/E/F)	50 miles/80km	E-/F-/G-band FCR for the SA-2 guideline (Sov S-75 Dvina), cued by P-12 Spoon Rest or P-15M Squat Eye	
SNR-125 (Low Blow)	56 miles/90km	engagement radar for the SA-3 Goa (Sov S-125 Neva) SAM, cued by P-12 Spoon Rest or P-15M Squat Eye	
NIIP 1S91 (Straight Flush)	43 miles/70km	mobile X-band engagement radar for SA-6 Gainful (Sov 2K12 Kub) SAM	
NII-20 1S51M3-2 (Land Roll)	19 miles/30km	TELAR-mounted H-J-band engagement radar for SA-8 Gecko (Sov 9K33 Osa) TELAR	
RPK-2 Tobol (Gun Dish)	5 miles/8km	fire control radar for the ZSU-23-4P 23mm SPAAG and the SA-9 (Sov 9K31 Strela 1) TELAR	
1S80 Sborka (Dog Ear)	23 miles/37km	acquisition radar for SA-13 (Sov 9K35 Strela-10)	
Roland	10 miles/16km	acquisition and tracking radars for Roland 1/2 TELAR	
1 EW/GCI = Early Warning/Ground Controlled Intercept 2 Tiger G license-built by Iraq as the SDA-G			

Though impressive in theory and on paper, the crucial weakness in the system was overreliance on a centralized and hierarchical Soviet-style approach to air defense, with the SOCs choosing

OPPOSITE IRAQI AIR DEFENCE SYSTEM

RIGHT
The Iraqi radar order of battle was formidable, its air defense forces fielding 16 different types of early warning/acquisition (EW/A) radars, 11 of Soviet origin and five of French. Here is a VNIIRT P-15 Trail (NATO Flat Face A) C-Band UHF early warning and acquisition radar capable of "seeing" for 140 miles (230km). Targeting such radars was a high Coalition priority. (DoD)

FAR RIGHT
This is an Egyptian SNR-75M3 (NATO Fan Song E) engagement radar, one of three SNR-75 variants (the others being the Fan Song B and F) Iraqi air defenders used to control S-75 family (NATO SA-2B/D/E/F Guideline) SAMs. The SNR-75/Fan Song FCR would be cued by a SKB P-12 Yenisei (NATO Spoon Rest B/C) or VNIIRT P-15M Trail (NATO Squat Eye) EW/A radar. (DoD)

the best engagement system (aircraft or SAM), and even the tactics of the intercept and numbers of missiles to fire, then passing this to the individual IOCs for execution. Therefore, Iraqi fighter pilots operated – like their Warsaw Pact counterparts – within a rigid and largely inflexible Ground Controlled Intercept (GCI) construct, and this influenced their training, leaving them seriously deficient compared to Coalition airmen, many of whom had honed their air combat skills in wide-ranging exercises such as Red Flag, Maple Flag, and the like. Worse, KARI was not a "balanced" system: oriented towards Israel and Iran, it had only limited coverage to the south, against Saudi Arabia, creating a corridor pointed right at Baghdad.

Air defenses

As of January 1991, the total number of known operational Iraqi surface-to-air missile (SAM) batteries included approximately 90 SA-2, SA-3, SA-6, and SA-8 batteries, and roughly the same number of French Roland 1/2 batteries. Most were clustered in a "point

The iconic Soviet S-75 (NATO SA-2 Guideline), ubiquitous throughout the Middle East and in the Communist world, formed an important component of the Iraqi air defense system. It could reach 82,000ft and had a range of over 28 miles (45km). Though the oldest of all Iraqi SAM systems, it was still deadly, claiming a USAF F-15E attacking Scud sites in Western Iraq and an RAF Tornado shot down attacking hardened aircraft shelters at al Taqaddum (Tammuz AB) on February 14, 1991. (DoD)

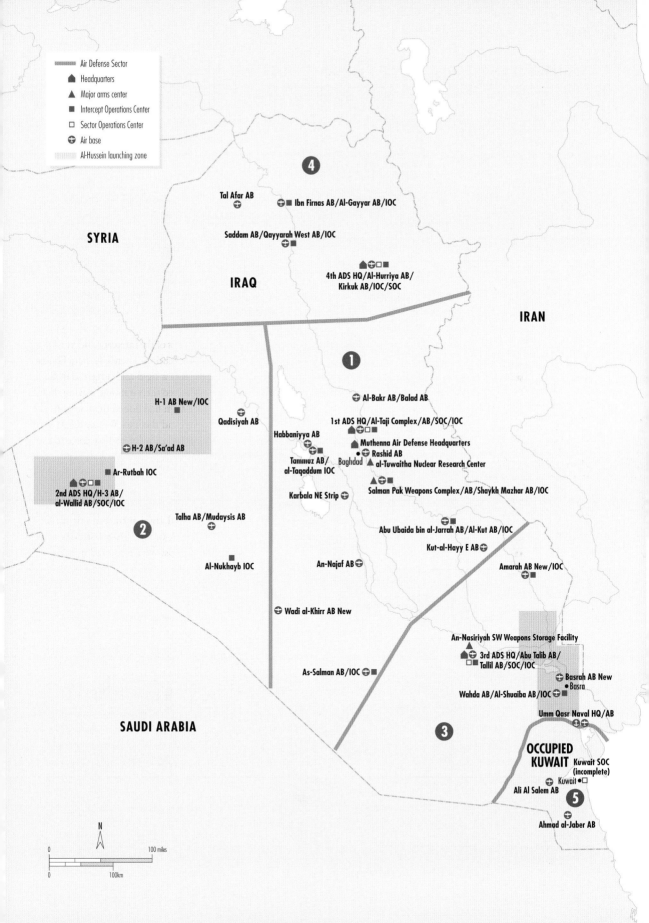

Air Defense Sector
- ▮ Air Defense Sector
- ⬟ Headquarters
- ▲ Major arms center
- ▪ Intercept Operations Center
- ☐ Sector Operations Center
- ✪ Air base
- ▨ Al-Hussein launching zone

SYRIA

IRAQ

IRAN

❹

Tal Afar AB ✪   ✪▪ Ibn Firnas AB/Al-Gayyar AB/IOC

Saddam AB/Qayyarah West AB/IOC ✪▪

⬟✪☐▪ 4th ADS HQ/Al-Hurriya AB/
Kirkuk AB/IOC/SOC

❶

✪ Al-Bakr AB/Balad AB

H-1 AB New/IOC ▪
                  ✪ Qadisiyah AB   1st ADS HQ/Al-Taji Complex/AB/SOC/IOC ⬟✪☐▪
                        Habbaniyya AB   ⬟ Muthenna Air Defense Headquarters
❚ H-2 AB/Sa'ad AB ✪   ✪▪ ● ✪ Rashid AB
                        Tammuz AB/   Baghdad ▲ al-Tuwaitha Nuclear Research Center
▪ Ar-Rutbah IOC   al-Taqaddum IOC   ▲✪▪
⬟✪☐▪   Karbala NE Strip ✪   Salman Pak Weapons Complex/AB/Shaykh Mazhar AB/IOC
2nd ADS HQ/H-3 AB/
al-Wallid AB/SOC/IOC
        ❷   ✪▪
                Talha AB/Mudaysis AB ✪   Abu Ubaida bin al-Jarrah AB/Al-Kut AB/IOC
                                          Kut-al-Hayy E AB ✪
        ▪   An-Najaf AB ✪
Al-Nukhayb IOC   Amarah AB New/IOC ✪
                                                        ▪

                ✪ Wadi al-Khirr AB New

                                    An-Nasiriyah SW Weapons Storage Facility
                                    ▲✪ 3rd ADS HQ/Abu Talib AB/
                                    ☐▪ Tallil AB/SOC/IOC
                As-Salman AB/IOC ✪▪
                                                ✪ Basrah AB New
                            Wahda AB/Al-Shuaiba AB/IOC ✪▪ ● Basra

SAUDI ARABIA   Umm Qasr Naval HQ/AB ✪
                                                        ✪✪
                            ❸
                                        OCCUPIED
                                        KUWAIT Kuwait SOC
                                                    (incomplete)
                                                ✪ Kuwait ●☐
                                        Ali Al Salem AB   ❺

                                                ✪
                                            Ahmad al-Jaber AB

N

0 _____ 100 miles
0 _____ 100km

A loaded Iraqi Vympel 2K12 Kub (NATO SA-6 Gainful) mobile SAM TEL (transporter-erector-launcher). The medium altitude SA-6 employed rocket-ramjet propulsion, and could reach 46,000ft (14km) with a range of 15 miles (24km).

The Soviet 9K-35 Strela-10 (NATO SA-13 Gopher) was a sophisticated low-altitude air defense missile system cued by a 1S80 Sborka (NATO Dog Ear) radar, capable of reaching an altitude of 11,500ft (3.5km), and having a range of 3.1 miles (5km). (DoD)

defense" strategy shielding key military establishments and sites such as the H-1/-2/-3 airfield complex, Mosul, Kirkuk, Amarah, Basra, and Nasiriyah, the Taji weapons complex, and particularly Baghdad. As well, every major Iraqi air base was protected by a missile brigade, and after the occupation of Kuwait, 14 SAM batteries were deployed across that tiny country to protect Iraqi ground forces. An estimated 3,679 SAMs were immediately available, not counting thousands more of man-portable (MANPADS) ones.

While the focus of the IrADF was strategic air defense (particularly, as noted, defense of Baghdad and critical weapons development centers), the focus of the Iraqi Army was tactical air defense of ground forces. To protect its fielded and mechanized forces from low-altitude attack, it possessed over 8,000 portable and mobile missile systems including SA-7 (Sov 9K32 Strela-2), SA-9 (Sov 9K31 Strela-1), SA-13 (Sov 9K35 Strela-10), and SA-14 (Sov 9K34 Strela-3); radar-cued Roland 1s and 2s, and SA-8 (Sov 9K33 Osa) mobile short-range missile systems.

Iraq had not only a layered air defense system, but a system in which antiaircraft cannon were typically employed alongside missile defenses. Iraq possessed over 2,400 emplaced AAA cannon – Baghdad alone had 1,267 guns distributed among 380 AAA sites – and more than 6,100 mobile AAA weapons. These ranged from heavy (14.5mm) machine guns through self-propelled antiaircraft guns (SPAAGs) such as the ZSU-23/4P Shilka self-propelled quad 23mm radar-directed antiaircraft system, and up to 130mm radar-directed KS-30 cannon. These covered from ground-level to over 40,000ft, though the most dangerous altitudes, not surprisingly, were from ground level up to 20,000ft, the band through which Iraqi air defense tacticians believed the Coalition would choose to fly. Iraq had 39 antiaircraft battalions equipped with just 37mm AAA cannon, including 26 regional, nine field defense, and four Republican Guard battalions.

In the words of the postwar American Title V Report *Conduct of the Persian Gulf Conflict*,

The Iraqi air defense system was formidable, combining the best features of several systems. The multi-layered, redundant, computer-controlled air defense network around Baghdad was more dense than that surrounding most Eastern European cities during the Cold War, and several orders of magnitude greater than that which had defended Hanoi during the later stages of the Vietnam War. If permitted to function as designed, the air defense array was capable of effective protection of key targets in Iraq.

That recognition drove Coalition planners as they strived to craft a winning air plan.

CAMPAIGN OBJECTIVES
Resolutions and resolve

The UN Security Council passed Resolution 660 on the day of the invasion, demanding Iraq's immediate withdrawal from Kuwait. On President Bush's orders, the nuclear carrier *Eisenhower* (CVN-69) and the carrier *Independence* (CV-62) steamed towards the Red Sea and North Arabian Sea. On August 4, Schwarzkopf (accompanied by a bleary-eyed Horner, who had worked through the night with only a 30-minute nap) helicoptered from the Pentagon to Camp David in the cool Maryland foothills. They briefed Bush on military options, and he conveyed his own concerns over casualties, stressing that, if war came, they should work to limit loss of life on both sides. "That provided the yardstick by which I measured later every one of our actions," Horner recalled.

On August 5, Bush emphatically stated that the Iraqi invasion "shall not stand," announcing four objectives: the immediate, complete, and unconditional withdrawal of all Iraqi forces from Kuwait; the restoration of Kuwait's legitimate government; the assurance of the security and stability of Saudi Arabia and the Persian Gulf; and the assurance of safety and protection of American citizens abroad.

That same day Cheney, undersecretary of defense Paul Wolfowitz, and Schwarzkopf flew to Saudi Arabia to meet with King Fahd. When asked on August 6 if he would permit the entry of American forces, he replied "Okay." Schwarzkopf turned to Horner and said "Chuck, start them moving." "Please God," Horner thought, "keep me from screwing things up."

By the end of the first week, the USAF had deployed ten fighter squadrons to the Gulf, a major contribution to stabilizing the crisis. "The squadrons of F-15 and F-16 fighter planes," Schwarzkopf recalled, "flowed to Saudi Arabia wonderfully." So, too, did troops and materiel: in the first 18 weeks, airlifters moved almost three times the entire payload carried in the Berlin airlift of 1948–49.

As junior officers, all the American senior commanders had fought in Southeast Asia, and all were outspoken about not wishing to repeat its failures. "To understand the success of *Desert Storm* you have to study Vietnam," Gen Chuck Horner said after the Gulf War,

As base personnel cheer and wave, the "Gorillas" of the 58th TFS, 33rd TFW taxi out at Eglin AFB, Florida, before taking off for deployment to Saudi Arabia. The 58th TFS would be the most successful fighter squadron in the Gulf War. In the foreground is a McDonnell-Douglas F-15C (SN 85-096), which as late as 2017 was still in service. (DoD)

Iraqi dictator Saddam Hussein and his senior staff stand with Yassar Arafat, Chairman of the Palestine Liberation Organization (PLO), in 1988. Both before and during the Gulf crisis, Arafat served the interests of Saddam, rationalizing his seizure of Kuwait and denying he posed any threat to Saudi Arabia and the other Gulf states. HRH Saudi General Khaled bin Sultan even believed Arafat, and in concert with Jordan's King Hussein and Yemen's President Ali Abdallah Salih "directly or indirectly" encouraged Saddam to invade Kuwait. (Courtesy of Hulton Archives, Getty Images 51630237)

Bottom (L– R): Prime Minister Margaret Thatcher, President George H.W. Bush, and NATO Secretary General Manfred Wörner (on the couch closest to Bush) meeting at the White House on August 6, 1990 to discuss the growing Gulf crisis. Left of Wörner on the couch is US Secretary of State James Baker; left of Baker is White House Chief of Staff John Sununu. On left couch, center, is Lt Gen Brent Scowcroft, USAF (ret.), GHWB's National Security Advisor. (George H.W. Bush Presidential Library and Museum)

adding, "That's where the lessons were learned – you don't learn from success, you learn from failure, and we had plenty of failure in Vietnam to study."

One was Washington's political and military elite dominating the targeting and tactical execution process; Horner on his very first Wild Weasel mission had nearly been killed because of a strike plan conceived in the White House meeting by individuals – including then-Secretary of Defense Robert S. McNamara – who were totally ignorant of the realities of North Vietnamese air defenses. Horner was determined that would never happen again, noting, "In Vietnam, the Secretary of Defense and the President selected our targets in the North. In *Desert Storm* the captains, majors, and lieutenant colonels – the war planners in the theater – selected them. We welcomed information and suggestions from any source, but target decisions would remain in theater with all being kept aware of the current plan."

On August 8, while still back in the States, Schwarzkopf had asked Gen John M. "Mike" Loh, the Air Force Vice Chief of Staff, for a strategic attack quick retaliation option if Saddam did something immediately, something egregious. Referencing current Army doctrine written to defeat a Warsaw Pact armoured thrust into Western Europe, Schwarzkopf said, "The air operations plans here are traditional Air–Land Battle scenarios but very little independent air operations that destroy strategic targets." Loh recalled, "I could hardly believe what I was hearing. Here was an Army commander talking like an air power advocate."

Loh turned to Col John A. Warden III, the service's leading air strategist and chief of "Checkmate," officially the Deputy Directorate for Warfighting Concepts. Warden and his staff, buttressed by planners from Tactical Air Command and Strategic Air Command, had already prepared a think-piece named *Instant Thunder* to pointedly draw a distinction between it and the feckless gradualism of Vietnam's *Rolling Thunder*. On Friday August 10, Warden briefed it to Schwarzkopf. Never given to understatement he proclaimed "You've restored my confidence in the Air Force," adding "Shit, I love it!" Next, Warden, supported by Loh, briefed it to Powell on Saturday August 11. As the Chairman listened, the two volleyed and beat back intense criticism from the J-3 Director of Operations, Army Lt Gen Thomas Kelly, who argued more with passion than with facts against having any air campaign prior to the invasion to liberate Kuwait itself. Afterwards, Powell told Warden it was a "good plan, very fine piece of work," but cautioned, "I won't be happy until I see those tanks destroyed," adding, "I want to leave smoking tanks as kilometer posts all the way to Baghdad." Next Warden left for Riyadh.

Though it won plaudits from Powell and Schwarzkopf, *Instant Thunder* did not go down well when Warden briefed it at a "very tense" two-hour meeting with Horner and his staff in Riyadh on August 20. To Horner, it was Vietnam redux, Washington running targeting, non-war-fighters playing at being war-fighters. As he listened, though, Horner recognized

brilliance underpinning it, considering it a "tremendous listing of targets and thoughts." But its almost exclusively strategic focus did not address his immediate problem: how to stop Iraq's armoured and mechanized divisions if they crossed the border. Worse, it divided up Air Force, Navy, and Marine air by geographical location, mirroring Vietnam's six Route Packages ("Route Packs"), fractionalizing air power, and derailing any unity of effort. Afterwards, he thanked Warden for coming by, kept three of his people, and called Brig Gen Buster C. Glosson (who had worked for him) to run the plans shop.

Glosson was deputy commander of Joint Task Force Middle East (JTFME) aboard the USS *La Salle*, an antenna-festooned command ship that spent most of its time tied up in port. Answering the phone, he thrilled to hear Horner's characteristic bark: "Get your ass up here now!" To Glosson the *La Salle* was "like a cocoon" leaving him "isolated and confined:" it was so bad he had earlier visited Horner, pleading "You have got to get me off this ship!"

A supremely confident, hard-driving, ambitious, aggressive, and tirelessly energetic former fighter wing commander, Glosson had a talent for cutting to the heart of issues and getting a job done. He cared deeply about his people and particularly the aircrew who would fly against Iraq, masking his feelings (which he confided to a diary) behind a combative and at times abrasive personality: no one was ever neutral about Buster Glosson, nor ever in doubt of where they stood in his eyes. He immediately left to take over campaign planning, assuming command as well of the 14th Air Division (Provisional). Now in charge of all of Horner's A-10s, F-15s, F-15Es, F-16s, F-111s, EF-111s, and F-117s – nearly 750 airplanes – he had almost miraculously gone from the depressing confines of a ship's cabin to become a veritable Fighter God.

The genesis of the air campaign plan predated the invasion of Kuwait, stemming from an emergency air response plan Horner had crafted earlier in 1990 and played out in a CENTCOM exercise, *Internal Look* 90. In that exercise (which presupposed an invasion of Saudi Arabia by Iraq, though the State Department insisted it be renamed in the exercise as the "State of Orange"), Horner had made use of existing capabilities and constructs – for example, the Saudi air defense network – and reimagined using other capabilities. He convinced Lt Gen John Yeosock, the ARCENT commander, to use the PAC-2 Patriot Army surface-to-air missile system to defend against Saddam's Scuds and Al-Husseins. He envisioned large-scale battlefield air interdiction. Once CENTCOM launched a counteroffensive, the air campaign would begin "Push CAS": close air support, but with a difference. Instead of having "dedicated" CAS aircraft on alert waiting for hours for calls that might not come, aircraft already airborne—even on other missions—would be immediately diverted to CAS if an emergency arose, a rapid and responsive "surge" of sorties streaming across the battle space in a continuous flow.

Marines from Camp Pendleton board a 437th AW C-141B Starlifter at Norton AFB, CA, for the long transit to Saudi Arabia. The C-141B was a stretch version of the Vietnam-era C-141A, and equipped – as a lesson learned from the 1973 Arab–Israeli war – with a receptacle for boom refueling, visible here as the bulge aft of the cockpit. (DoD)

Fighter God: Brig Gen Buster Glosson, Horner's Chief of Campaign Plans, in the Black Hole. (DoD from Lt Gen David A. Deptula USAF (ret.) Collection)

VADM Stan Arthur worked miracles getting NAVCENT ready for a war due to erupt just a little over six weeks after he arrived in theater. A highly experienced light attack pilot with a distinguished combat record, Arthur recognized that Horner's Air Tasking Order (ATO) process, cumbersome though it may be, constituted the only means to organize, deconflict, and control the thousands of daily sorties flying into Iraq and Kuwait. He instructed his two carrier task force commanders to make certain their over-land flight operations were integrated within it and that their airmen were familiar with it. (DoD)

Like many good commanders, Horner was neither a meddler nor a micromanager, and he left Glosson and his planning staff generally free to craft their plans, only insisting that the air campaign had to be a unified one. For this reason, he blew up in an August 1990 meeting with VADM Henry H. Mauz Jr, then CENTCOM's NAVCENT. VADM Mauz, an outstanding officer who later commanded the Navy's Atlantic Fleet, was not a naval aviator. Ignorant of how bitterly Vietnam-era Air Force, Navy, and Marine airmen regarded dividing up air power according to geography, he blithely proposed dividing Kuwait and Iraq into Route Packs, with the Navy taking some and the Air Force taking others. "I said to him, 'Admiral, if you try and pull that bullshit, I will retire before I'll agree to it,'" Horner told this author in 2011 – Mauz recalls an earthier response beginning "F--- that!" – and with that, Route Packs died for good.

Mauz, already due for reassignment, left CENTCOM at the beginning of December 1990, replaced by VADM Stanley "Stan" Arthur. A highly decorated light attack A-4 pilot who, like Horner, had flown during *Rolling Thunder*, Arthur had no desire to repeat the Route Pack experience, and, in the words of the official naval history, "made smoothing over any remaining rough edges with Horner a top priority." Subsequently, Arthur and Horner worked together extremely well, Buster Glosson considering Arthur "a gem: bright, a straight-shooter, and easy to work with even on the toughest of issues," and Horner recollecting that he "fully appreciated the need for a single commander for air, no matter what service uniform he wore."

More importantly still, Arthur, after meeting with Schwarzkopf, realized that campaign planning had gone far beyond what NAVCENT's personnel – headquartered by their own choice down in Bahrain and thus far from Riyadh – realized: war was imminent, not just a remote possibility to plan for. "Frustrated and disappointed" at the "immature" state of NAVCENT's war planning, Arthur immediately focused his efforts on getting it and, particularly, the two carrier battle fleets in the Red Sea and Gulf waters ready for war, reorganizing NAVCENT's command structure and – very importantly – increasing its staff representation in Riyadh. As for the air campaign, he put two very fine officers in the Black Hole, a secure area in the basement of RSAF headquarters in Riyadh, to liaise with Buster Glosson and his planners.

MARCENT and First Marine Expeditionary Force (I MEF) commander Lt Gen Walt Boomer, reflecting the views of his senior Marine aviator, Maj Gen Royal N. Moore (deputy commander of I MEF and commander of the 3rd Marine Air Wing based at Al Jubayl) pushed back against the whole JFACC concept. Their position was that Horner could "coordinate" Marine air, but could never "command" it. (Indeed, MARCENT paperwork often referred to the JFACC as the "Joint Force Air Component *Coordinator*.") Though this ran counter to Schwarzkopf's guidance to Buster Glosson (viz. "If you aren't part of the air campaign under Horner, you don't fly"), Horner, by nature pragmatic and focused on results, let it slide, and, in fact, really didn't care: he had a huge amount of available Air Force and Coalition air, and as long as the Marine air effort supported Schwarzkopf's goals as CINCCENT, and their sorties showed up on the Master Attack Plan and the daily Air Tasking Order, things would be just fine. Indeed, the Saudis insisted from the beginning of the Gulf crisis that any military airplane from any service or nation overflying Saudi Arabia had to be in the ATO, whether on training or an operational sortie.

Overall, Horner had a high regard for his CENTCOM colleagues and their foreign equivalents, remarking shortly after the war that "The four of us – Walt Boomer, Stan Arthur, John Yeosock, and myself – were like brothers. We would never try to do anything to one another." He was not one to engage in feuds, hold grudges, or to remind others of their failings, remarking, "You don't make money rubbing salt in open wounds."

The conceptual framework guiding the planning process was Schwarzkopf's own: a four-phase series of mini-campaigns.

Phase I would be a strategic air campaign over Iraq to gain air superiority, and destroy Iraqi strategic capabilities including Nuclear, Biological, Chemical (NBC), and Scuds, and to disrupt Iraqi Command and Control (C2).

Phase II SEAD attacks over Kuwait to Suppress Enemy Air Defenses in the KTO.

Phase III Attriting enemy ground power while continuing to service Phase I and II targets as needed, and shifting air attack emphasis to the fielded Iraqi forces in Kuwait.

Phase IV support of ground operations during the liberation of Kuwait.

It was Schwarzkopf, then, an Army non-aviator, who determined air would spearhead the campaign as the sole, or at least the dominant, combat arm in the war's first three phases. "He really was a profound individual," Horner told this author in 2011, "very smart, one who appreciated what air could do for everyone."

Glosson's planning staff resided in the Black Hole. Altogether it eventually grew to 55 individuals, organized into four distinct groupings, each with both a day and night team so that its operations would be seamless and continuous:

Guidance, Apportionment, and Targeting (GAT), responsible for two mini-cells, Iraqi Planning and Kuwaiti Theater of Operations (KTO) Planning, which addressed Nuclear, Biological, and Chemical (NBC) targeting and Scuds; and Iraq's Integrated Air Defense System (IADS) including airfields, aircraft, SAMs, AAA, and Electronic Combat (EC). Out of this came the Master Attack Plan (MAP).

Air Tasking Order (ATO), responsible for building the daily ATO that governed combat operations.

Airborne Command Element (ACE), which oversaw the execution of combat operations, consisting of four teams airborne in airborne command posts.

Component Liaison (LNO), consisting of liaison officers from partner air forces and sister services assigned to the Black Hole, including the Saudis, British, French, Canadians, Italians, the two Navy carrier strike forces, the Marines, the Army, and Special Operations Command.

The planners constituted a galaxy of talent, including Brig Gen Larry "Poobah" Henry, the West's leading expert on taking down Soviet-style integrated air defense systems and electronic combat; Col Anthony J. "Tony" Tolin, former commander of the super-secret F-117A "stealth"

On October 17, 1990, Air Force Secretary Donald B. Rice visited CENTCOM. Here he is shown with 13 of the 54-person Black Hole air campaign planning team. L–R: Capt Mike "Cos" Cosby, Wg Cdr Mick Richardson RAF, Maj John Kinser, Lt Gen Chuck Horner, Maj Scott Hente, Lt Col Bert Pryor, Capt Bill "Burners" Bruner, Maj Jeff "Oly" Olsen, Lt Col Rodgers Greenawalt, Maj John Turk, Sgt Barbe, Maj Bob Eskridge, SECAF Don Rice, Lt Col Dave Deptula, Brig Gen Buster Glosson. (DoD from Deptula Collection)

OPPOSITE COALITION AIR BASES IN *DESERT STORM*

fighters; Col Jeffrey S. "Fang" Feinstein, a WSO F-4 ace from the Vietnam War; Lt Col David "Zatar" Deptula, a brilliant air strategist and principal author of the Air Force's *Global Reach–Global Power* strategic planning framework; Lt Col Richard "Rick" Lewis, who would develop the innovative "Kill Box/Killer Scout" concept used in the KTO; Lt Col Sam Baptiste, an expert on battlefield air power application who would oversee KTO planning for Phase III and Phase IV; Maj Mark "Buck" Rogers, an expert in apportionment and attrition; and Wing Commander Mick Richardson of the RAF who, early on, had volunteered his services to the planners.

Working with the planning team were experts from various weapon system communities, such as the F-117, B-52, F-15E, and so on, other US and Coalition service representatives, and other Coalition commanders and key staff including Lt Gen Ahmad al-Buhairi (RSAF); AVM William Wratten (RAF); Maj Gen Claude Solanet (French AF); Maj Gen Mario Arpino (Italian AF); Lt Col Abdullah al-Samdan (Kuwait); and Lt Col John McNeil (Canadian Air Command). "Eventually we opened the doors to all members of the coalition: the Bahrainis, Saudis, Kuwaitis, everyone had full access and it paid off," Horner noted after the war.

The Black Hole also had access to outside experts in the American intelligence community and in sister services. Back in the Pentagon, Col John Warden worked tirelessly to ensure the Black Hole's bomb damage assessments and other intelligence needs were met; so, too, did the Joint Staff J-2 (Intelligence), RADM John M. "Mike" McConnell, whose careful analyses, balanced judgment, and constant contact with Horner and Glosson materially assisted air campaign planning and execution. Finally, Capt J. Michael "Carlos" Johnson, director of the Navy's SPEAR (Strike Projection Evaluation and Anti-Air Research) naval air intelligence staff who furnished assessments of Iraqi air defense capabilities.

The final campaign plan crafted out of this took Schwarzkopf's four-phase campaign plan and effectively filled it with actions against 12 key target sets totaling (as of mid-December 1990) 237 targets:

Iraqi strategic air defense (Crack the French-built KARI Integrated Air Defense System on the war's opening night by a mix of Stealth attacks on headquarters, control, and operations centers; "soft kill" communications and radar jamming; threat deception to trigger radar illumination; "hard kills" against threat radars by Coalition HARM and ALARM shooters; and Special Operations Forces (SOF); jam, engage, and destroy intercepting Iraqi fighter aircraft)

Leadership command facilities (Strike Political–Military headquarters, command posts, key government offices, in total a 45-target set);

Nuclear and chemical-biological weapons research, production, and storage (Attack with bunker-shattering blast and highly energetic munitions to shatter research and production facilities and to burn CBW stocks)

Scud (Al Hussein) theater ballistic missiles (Target fixed launch sites in western Iraq's H-2/H-3 complexes; destroy research, development, test, and production facilities; hunt mobile Scud TELs with airborne and SOF assets; defend against Scud launches with a mix of warning, protective gear, shelters, and PAC-2 Patriot terminal defense)

Republican Guard (RG) and Iraqi Fielded Forces in the Kuwaiti Theater of Operations (KTO) (The RG constituted a priority Kuwaiti Theater of Operations target repeatedly emphasized by CINCCENT Schwarzkopf – though, as he himself said in the midst of the war, "'elite' is a relative word" – the RG posed a threat that warranted persistent, continuous attacks, with other formations to be targeted as well by Coalition bombers, fighter-bombers, and tank-killers)

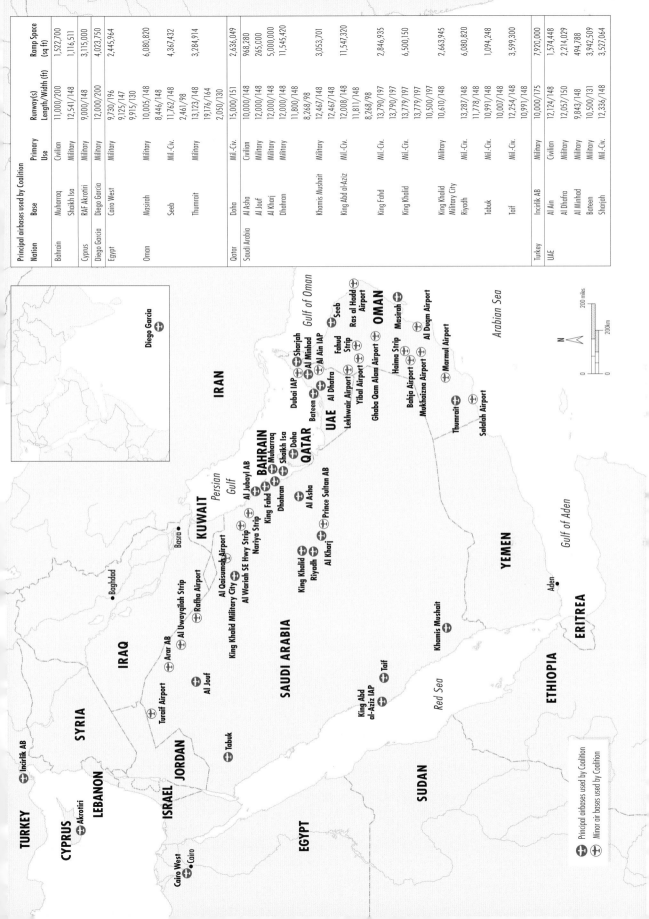

Principal airbases used by Coalition				
Nation	Base	Primary Use	Runway(s) Length/Width (ft)	Ramp Space (sq ft)
Bahrain	Muharraq	Civilian	11,000/200	1,522,700
	Shaikh Isa	Military	12,541/148	1,116,511
Cyprus	RAF Akrotiri	Military	9,000/148	3,115,000
Diego Garcia	Diego Garcia	Military	12,000/200	4,023,750
Egypt	Cairo West	Military	9,730/196 9,125/147 9,915/130	2,445,964
Oman	Masirah	Military	10,005/148	6,080,820
	Seeb	Mil.-Civ.	8,446/148	4,367,432
	Thumrait	Military	11,762/148 2,461/98 13,123/148 19,176/164 2,050/130	3,284,914
Qatar	Doha	Mil.-Civ.	15,000/151	2,636,049
Saudi Arabia	Al Asha	Civilian	10,000/148	968,280
	Al Jouf	Military	12,000/148	265,000
	Al Kharj	Military	12,000/148	5,000,000
	Dhahran	Military	12,000/148 11,800/148 8,268/98	11,545,420
	Khamis Mushait	Military	12,467/148 12,467/148	3,053,701
	King Abd al-Aziz	Mil.-Civ.	12,008/148 11,811/148 8,268/98	11,547,320
	King Fahd	Mil.-Civ.	13,790/197 13,790/197	2,846,935
	King Khalid	Mil.-Civ.	13,779/197 13,779/197	6,500,150
	King Khalid Military City	Military	10,500/197 10,610/148	2,663,945
	Riyadh	Mil.-Civ.	13,287/148	6,080,820
	Tabuk	Mil.-Civ.	11,778/148 10,991/148	1,094,248
	Taif	Mil.-Civ.	10,007/148 12,254/148 10,991/148	3,599,300
Turkey	Incirlik AB	Military	10,000/175	7,920,000
UAE	Al Ain	Civilian	12,124/148	1,574,448
	Al Dhafra	Military	12,057/150	2,214,029
	Al Minhad	Military	9,843/148	494,788
	Bateen	Military	10,500/131	3,942,509
	Sharjah	Mil.-Civ.	12,336/148	3,527,064

TURKEY
Incirlik AB

CYPRUS
Akrotiri

LEBANON

SYRIA

ISRAEL

JORDAN

IRAQ
Baghdad
Turaif Airport
Arar AB
Al Uwayqilah Strip
Rafha Airport

EGYPT
Cairo West
Cairo

SAUDI ARABIA
Tabuk
Al Jouf
King Abd al-Aziz IAP
Taif
King Khalid Military City
Al Qaisumah Airport
Al Wariah SE Hwy Strip
Nariya Strip
King Fahd
King Khalid
Riyadh
Al Kharj
Khamis Mushait

KUWAIT
Basra

Persian Gulf

BAHRAIN
Muharraq
Shaikh Isa
Al Jubayl AB
Dhahran
Al Asha
Prince Sultan AB

QATAR
Doha

UAE
Dubai IAP
Sharjah
Al Minhad
Bateen
Al Ain IAP
Al Dhafra
Lekhwair Airport
Yibal Airport
Ghaba Qam Alam Airport
Bahja Airport
Mukhaizna Airport
Marmul Airport
Al Duqm Airport
Salalah Airport
Thumrait

OMAN
Fahud Strip
Seeb
Ras al Hadd Airport
Haima Strip
Masirah

Gulf of Oman

Arabian Sea

IRAN

RED SEA
Red Sea

SUDAN

ETHIOPIA

ERITREA

YEMEN
Aden

Gulf of Aden

N

0   200 miles
0   200km

Principal airbases used by Coalition
Minor air bases used by Coalition

Telecommunications and command, control, and communications (C3) (Undertake persistent attacks to destroy microwave relay towers, telephone exchanges, switching rooms, fiberoptic cable nodes, and bridges that carried coaxial communications cables)

Electrical production and distribution (Targeted attacks by TLAM, CALCM, and other strikers)

Oil refining and distribution (Target short-term military refined POL production, storage, and distribution, not long-term crude oil production, by striking cracking and distillation towers and complexes)

Railroads and bridges (Exploit the power of precision attack to sever Iraqi lines of communication (LOCs) by dropping vehicle and railroad bridges, thus reducing the Iraqi Army's ability to both move and resupply itself)

Airfields (Destroy/immobilize the IrAF by shattering runways, taxiways, hardened aircraft shelters, maintenance and storage facilities, and by fighter sweeps; prevent relocation of IrAF aircraft in Jordan);

Naval Forces and Naval Ports (Sink or incapacitate Iraq's missile boats and mine-layers; destroy shore-based antishipping missile launch facilities)

Military support, production, and storage (Destroy the most threatening arms dumps and then others that might be discovered)

In early October, Schwarzkopf sent Glosson and an Army team to brief Powell and the White House on the air and ground plans his airmen and soldiers were working on. Glosson's briefing unsettled Powell, who said, "I don't want the President [Bush] to grab onto that air campaign as a solution to everything." Then, amazingly, an *Air Force* general on the Joint Staff working for Powell took Glosson aside and said, "Your air campaign plan is too good; the Chairman is afraid the President will tell us to execute," recommending that when Glosson briefed the President he should "go through the plan much faster *and not be so convincing.*" Glosson curtly dismissed the advice, and, after being pinged a third time to tone it down, called back to Schwarzkopf who told him "in very direct fashion" to proceed as planned. Subsequently his briefing to Bush went very well, the old carrier pilot asking "many insightful questions."

On December 20, Secretary of Defense Cheney, JCS Chairman Powell, and Undersecretary of Defense Paul Wolfowitz – the latter a strong proponent of air power – attended a series of briefings with Schwarzkopf and the CENTCOM staff. Horner briefed the air campaign, which by then had undergone some revision: Phase III now had two parts, a Phase III Part A focus on the Republican Guard and a Phase III Part B focus on the Iraqi Army. The briefing went well, the plan by then effectively complete.

On December 20, SecDef Dick Cheney and JCS Chairman Gen Colin Powell met in Riyadh with Schwarzkopf and his senior staff to review war planning and preparations.(L–R, front) Gen Colin Powell USA, Chairman JCS; SecDef Dick Cheney; Gen Norman Schwarzkopf USA; CINC CENTCOM. Lt Gen Calvin Waller USA, Dep CINC CENTCOM. (L–R, back): Lt Gen Walt Boomer, MARCENT; Lt Gen Chuck Horner, JFACC / CENTAF; Lt Gen John Yeosock, ARCENT; VADM Stan Arthur, NAVCENT; Col Jesse Johnson, SOCCENT. Note the covered map on the back wall, so as to prevent any hint of the plan. (DoD)

THE CAMPAIGN
42 days to Kuwait City

When January 15, 1991 passed without Iraqi troops leaving Kuwait, President Bush issued National Security Directive 54, authorizing force to expel them. Chairman of the JCS Gen Colin Powell, brought Secretary of Defense Dick Cheney the "execute" order. Cheney signed it, and asked Powell to do so as well. There was a sense of moral right: Britain's Lt Gen Peter de la Billière recalled, "We were all facing a criminal lunatic who cared nothing for his own people and was prepared to sacrifice them by the thousand for his own glorification."

Final countdown

On the afternoon of January 15, Gen Schwarzkopf went to the Black Hole for a final Master Attack Plan briefing from Horner, Glosson, and Deptula. It went well until he asked, "Where are the B-52 strikes on the Republican Guard?" Told that Buffs weren't hitting the Guard on the opening night because of the dense and redundant SAM risk over Kuwait, the infamously mercurial Schwarzkopf erupted like a long-dormant volcano, shouting "You guys have lied to me!" As he raved, Glosson asked, "How many B-52s are you willing to lose?" Deptula started lecturing on the risks to Buffs from SAMs, then concluded it was "probably best to pause and let Gen Horner answer this one." Schwarzkopf's rage filled the room and, standing to the side, Maj Mark "Buck" Rogers, who ran Glosson's Guidance, Apportioning, and Targeting (GAT) cell, thought with bleak humor, "This is going well!" Fortunately, Horner saved the briefing, taking Schwarzkopf into his office and quietly reviewing each chart, emphasizing the Buffs would attack the Guard the moment they could safely do so. Schwarzkopf cooled down almost as rapidly as he had heated up, even apologizing for his outburst. It was the only time he blew up at his air campaign team, but despite his apology, "it left," as Glosson recollected, "an everlasting scar."

A Boeing B-52G Stratofortress of the 1708th Bomb Wing (Provisional) takes off from Jeddah on a *Desert Storm* bombing mission. B-52Gs only constituted three percent of total combat aircraft, but they dropped 72,000 bombs (totaling 27,000 tons) on a wide range of targets, roughly a third of all American tonnage dropped in the war. (DoD)

Storm before the Storm: Lt Col Dave Deptula briefs Gen Schwarzkopf in the Black Hole on the air campaign plan, January 15, 1991, minutes before Schwarzkopf erupted over the issue of B-52G strikes on the Republican Guard. (L–R): Lt Gen Horner, Brig Gen Glosson, Gen Schwarzkopf, and Lt Col Deptula. (DoD from Deptula Collection)

"Execute Wolfpack:" launching the Gulf War's most consequential air strikes

Afterwards, at 0600L in Riyadh on January 16, Horner sent a Coalition-wide alert to airmen, and at 1200L, he issued "Execute Wolfpack," commencing Phase I of the air campaign: H-Hour was set for 0000Z, 0300L Baghdad time, in the early morning of January 17.

Back in the United States, it was just after 0400 Washington time, and 0300 at Barksdale Air Force Base, Louisiana. There, as a picked team of maintainers readied their aircraft, seven select B-52G crews of Strategic Air Command's 2nd Bomb Wing were starting their final pre-mission briefing for what would be, at that time, the longest non-stop military air strike in aviation history, Operation *Senior Surprise*. Dubbed "Secret Squirrel" by its crews (so they could refer to it openly), it launched just over three hours later, at 0636 (1536L in Riyadh). Then, mission commander Lt Col John "Jay" Beard, CO of the 596th Bomb Squadron, and Crew S-91 under Capt Michael G. Wilson, thundered smokily down Barksdale's runway in B-52G *Petie 3rd,* call-sign Doom 31, leading six other Buffs into a rainy sky. They swiftly disappeared in the murk and clouds, the first combat mission launched in *Desert Storm*. Altogether they carried 39 Boeing AGM-86C Conventional Air Launched Cruise Missiles (CALCMs), a highly classified weapon, to help shatter Iraq's electrical grid by hitting eight key targets including the al Musayyib Thermal Power Plant, and transmission facilities at Mosul.

At sea, ashore, and at Diego Garcia, maintainers readied aircraft and weapons; aircrews suited up, checked their survival gear and sidearms, attended final briefings and reviewed their place in the campaign's first ATO; engines burst into life, aircraft taxied out and, after final "last chance" checks, accelerated down runways and into the night. There was no moon; it would rise at 0817L on January 17, not quite an hour after sunrise. At 2309Z (2009L in Riyadh) on January 16, 18 B-52Gs from SAC's 4300 BW (P) on Diego Garcia roared aloft; five "air spares" soon returned to base, leaving 13 pregnant with bombs bound for Iraq. Then, at midnight, Schwarzkopf issued "Execute Order – USCINCCENT OPORD 001 for Desert Storm."

In advance of the scheduled H-Hour of 0300, there were two "prequel" attacks. Shortly before 0100L on January 17, four Air Force MH-53J Pave Low helicopters and eight Army AH-64A Apache gunships completed engine run-ups, communications checks, and taxied out to the runway at Al Jouf, a forward operating base in northwest Saudi Arabia; right on the hour, they took off to attack border radar sites. At 0022L, the first of two dozen F-117As from the 37th TFW (P) left Khamis Mushait (dubbed "Tonopah East") to strike sector air defense, interceptor operations centers, other command and control, and leadership targets across Iraq and Baghdad.

At 0100L, Horner went to the Tactical Air Control Center (TACC), recalling the wait to H-Hour as "the worst minutes of my life." Privately he worried whether the F-117A – upon which so much depended – would live up to its pre-war hype: analysts had told Tactical Air Command's Gen Robert "Bob" Russ to expect to lose as many as one in every seven. Glosson asked how many Coalition aircraft Horner thought might be lost. Horner, thinking only of the USAF, scribbled "42." (Overall he thought Coalition losses might reach 100 airplanes.)

By now, Secret Squirrel's Barksdale Buffs were nearing Libya, on track to reach their launch sites over the western Saudi desert. In the Red Sea and Gulf, four carriers from VADM Stan Arthur's two CTF's – *Saratoga*, *Kennedy*, *Midway*, and *Ranger* – were poised to launch their

The "Secret Squirrel Seven's" Senior Surprise

On January 16, 1991, at 0636 local time, mission commander Lt Col John "Jay" Beard, aircraft commander Capt Michael G. Wilson, co-pilot 1Lt Kent R. Beck, and Crew S-91 lifted their massive eight-engine Boeing B-52G Stratofortress SN 58-0177 *Petie 3rd*, call-sign Doom 31, off the runway at Barksdale Air Force Base, Louisiana. Climbing smokily into rainy skies, six more thundering Buffs of the USAF Strategic Air Command's 596th Bomb Squadron, 2nd Bomb Wing, 8th Air Force followed them aloft.

Thus began Operation *Senior Surprise*, a highly classified mission its aircrew dubbed "Secret Squirrel," after a cartoon crime-fighter. The bombers were off to destroy portions of Iraq's electrical grid and communications infrastructure by attacking eight key targets with 39 long-range precision cruise missiles.

Beneath each airplane's inner wings were pylons mounting streamlined gray shapes looking like slab-sided fuel tanks. They were, instead, Boeing AGM-86C Conventional Air-Launched Cruise Missiles. The CALCM was a top-secret special access codeword-shielded weapon. Boeing had developed a short-range subsonic cruise missile, the AGM-86A, in the late 1970s, and then had stretched it, producing the long-range nuclear-armed AGM-86B. In turn, it spawned a non-nuclear derivative, the AGM-86C CALCM, with a 1,000lb special-purpose warhead. Powered by a Williams F107-WR-10 turbofan producing 600lb (2.67kN) of thrust, the CALCM had an effective range up to 1,000 miles, flying at low altitude, relying on both terrain-masking and its small visible and radar signatures to shield it from enemy fire. Unlike terrain-matching cruise missiles, it found its way using an onboard Global Positioning System (GPS) satellite navigation system.

Aboard the bombers were 57 aircrew. Six of the B-52Gs carried eight, the regular six-person pilot, co-pilot, radar navigator, navigator, electronic warfare officer, and tail gunner being augmented by another pilot and another navigator. The seventh B-52G, with a second augmentee pilot, had nine crew aboard.

After takeoff, the B-52Gs crossed the southern US, passed over the Atlantic, southern Europe, the Mediterranean, then down to the Red Sea and into western Saudi Arabia. They refueled multiple times, supported by 38 KC-135 tanker sorties out of Lajes Air Base, Azores, and 19 KC-10 tanker sorties from Morón Air Base, Spain. Early on January 17, the Buffs arrived over two launch areas 60 miles south of the Iraqi border between Al Jouf and Ar'ar. Pre-launch checks failed four missiles, but the other 35 were healthy, and so each aircraft launched its load. Last to strike was B-52G SN 58-0185 El Lobo II, Doom 37, flown by Capt Stephen D. Sicking and Crew S-93.

While one CALCM descended and crashed into the Saudi desert, the others continued onwards at low altitude, and of these, 28 hit their targets including the al-Musayyib Thermal Power Plant. SAC intelligence analysts concluded six targets ceased operation, one other was damaged, and one remained untouched.

As for the bombers, the "Secret Squirrel Seven" turned back to the United States, where, after facing dauntingly stiff headwinds and bad weather, they all safely returned between 33.9 hours and 35.4hrs after take-off, having completed (what was at that time) the longest strategic attack mission in aviation history.

Senior Surprise/Secret Squirrel blended all the qualities of modern air power: speed, range, flexibility, precision, and lethality. It thus constituted a fitting demonstration of the Air Force's new Global Reach–Global Power strategic planning concept issued in June 1990.

The artwork shows Sicking's El Lobo II launching Secret Squirrel's last CALCM, with one of the four failed missiles still locked on its pylon. El Lobo II is now exhibited at the Air Force Armament Museum, Eglin AFB, Florida.

OPPOSITE SMASHING IRAQ'S AIR DEFENSE SYSTEM

first strikes. Twenty Air Force F-15Cs from the 1st TFW (P), 4th TFW (P), and 33rd TFW (P) headed north from Dhahran, Al Kharj, and Tabuk. RSAF F-15Cs and RAF Tornado F.3s "capped" tankers and command and control aircraft over Saudi Arabia. Nineteen 4th TFW (P) F-15Es departed Al Kharj to strike five fixed Al Hussein launch sites in western Iraq.

F-111Fs from the 48th TFW (P) left Taif to attack Ad Diwaniyah, Ahmad Al Jaber, Ali Al Salem, Balad (al-Bakr), H-3, Jalibah, and Salman Pak (Shaykh Mazhar) air bases and chemical warfare sites, relying on eight PPN-19 navigation beacons and radar reflectors placed along the Saudi–Iraqi border by an Air Force–Army special operations team to update the F-111Fs' navigation systems.

RAF Tornado GR.1s and crews drawn from nine squadrons – IX, 14, XV, 16, 17, 20, 27, 31, and 617 – departed Dhahran, Muharraq, and Tabuk, bound for Tallil (Abu Talib AB), Mudaysis (Talha AB), Qadisiyah (al-Asad AB), and al-Taqaddum (Tammuz AB); a second wave would reattack Qadisiyah, Mudaysis, and strike Abu Ubaida Ibn al Jarrah (al-Kut-al Hayy AB), Wahda (al-Shuaiba AB), Wadi al-Khirr New AB, and H-3 (al-Wallid AB). Screening these were jammers, HARM and ALARM radar-killers, Northrop BQM-74C Chukar radar spoofers, and ADM-141A Tactical Air Launched Decoys (TALD).

New constellations appeared in the clear desert sky: over 160 tankers dragging long strings of aircraft visible by their navigation lights. After refueling, the lights winked out: they were off to war, visible only as ghostly green images seen through night vision goggles (NVG). "I thought it was fantastic," said then-Wg Cdr Jeremy "Jerry" Witts. Bound for Mudaysis (Talha AB) and leading four Tornado GR.1s, he marveled at the "hundreds and hundreds of planes up there – we were going to stuff this bloke and he deserved it."

At 0120L RADM Riley Mixon's Battle Force Yankee went to war: the *Kennedy* (CV-67) launched CVW-3's first air strike. Ten minutes later, at approximately 0130L, the Red Sea cruiser USS *San Jacinto* (CG-56) loosed the first shipboard cruise missile launched "in anger" in naval history, a General Dynamics BGM-109 Tomahawk TLAM-C; minutes later, more roared aloft from ships in the Arabian Gulf, the first "shots" of *Desert Storm*. America was now at war, no turning back.

At 0200L, RADM Daniel March's Battle Force Zulu joined in, *Ranger* (CV-61) launching CVW-2's first strike, a mixed force of bombers attacking the Umm Qasr naval base and its

The Sikorsky MH-53J Pave Low III, heir to the legendary HH-3E and HH-53B/C Jolly Greens of the Vietnam era, was virtually an afterthought in USAF 1970s and 1980s acquisition, but proved a stalwart of Air Force special operations for many decades. Robust, armored, and weaponized, it had advanced avionics and sensors – especially FLIR and GPS – that made it ideally suited for SOF pathfinding and insertion/ extraction, flown by crews whose skill was exceeded only by their courage. (DoD)

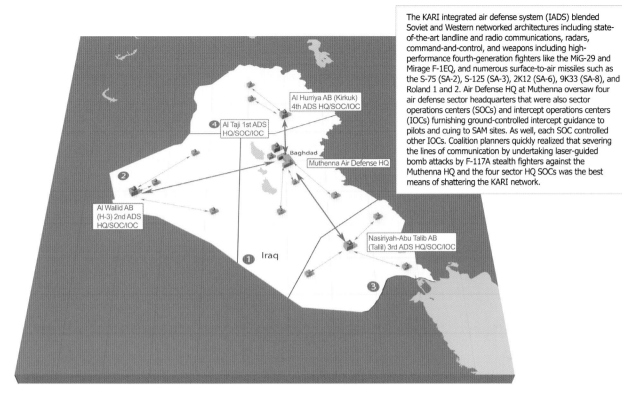

The KARI integrated air defense system (IADS) blended Soviet and Western networked architectures including state-of-the-art landline and radio communications, radars, command-and-control, and weapons including high-performance fourth-generation fighters like the MiG-29 and Mirage F-1EQ, and numerous surface-to-air missiles such as the S-75 (SA-2), S-125 (SA-3), 2K12 (SA-6), 9K33 (SA-8), and Roland 1 and 2. Air Defense HQ at Muthenna oversaw four air defense sector headquarters that were also sector operations centers (SOCs) and intercept operations centers (IOCs) furnishing ground-controlled intercept guidance to pilots and cuing to SAM sites. As well, each SOC controlled other IOCs. Coalition planners quickly realized that severing the lines of communication by undertaking laser-guided bomb attacks by F-117A stealth fighters against the Muthenna HQ and the four sector HQ SOCs was the best means of shattering the KARI network.

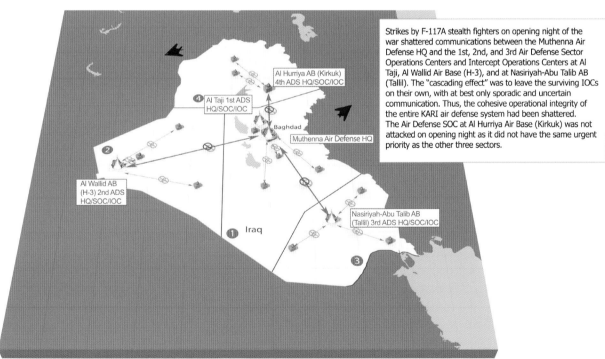

Strikes by F-117A stealth fighters on opening night of the war shattered communications between the Muthenna Air Defense HQ and the 1st, 2nd, and 3rd Air Defense Sector Operations Centers and Intercept Operations Centers at Al Taji, Al Wallid Air Base (H-3), and at Nasiriyah-Abu Talib AB (Tallil). The "cascading effect" was to leave the surviving IOCs on their own, with at best only sporadic and uncertain communication. Thus, the cohesive operational integrity of the entire KARI air defense system had been shattered. The Air Defense SOC at Al Hurriya Air Base (Kirkuk) was not attacked on opening night as it did not have the same urgent priority as the other three sectors.

 Muthenna Air Defense HQ

Air Defense Sector HQs (Sector Operations Centers, SOC)

 Intercept Operations Centers (IOC)

 Severed ADHQ-SOC Comm Node

 Severed SOC-IOC Comm Node

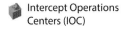 Muthenna ADHQ-SOC Comm Line

 SOC-IOC Comm Line

 F-117A Strike

 Number of Air Defense Sector

naval headquarters, and HARM-shooters to suppress radars. Maj Gen Royal Moore's Marines launched at 0230L, when A-6Es, EA-6Bs, and F/A-18s left Shaikh Isa to attack airfields, command and control, and Al-Hussein facilities at Wahda (al-Shuaiba AB), Tallil (Abu Talib AB), Qurnah, al-Rumaylah, al-Amarah, and Basra.

"Party in ten:" Operation Eager Anvil / Task Force Normandy

Far to the west, at 0212L, flying northeast of Ar'ar, the USAF MH-53J and ArmyAH-64 helicopters, now in two six-helicopter formations named Red Team and White Team, thrummed across the Saudi–Iraqi border at 50ft, opening Operation *Eager Anvil*, also known as Task Force Normandy. Each paired four Army AH-64A Apache gunships from Lt Col Dick Cody's 101st Aviation Regiment with two Air Force MH-53J Pave Low III pathfinders from Lt Col Rich Comer's 20th Special Operations Squadron.

Two radar sites guarded Iraq's western missile fields. Each had a mix of P-12 Spoon Rest, P-15 Flat Face, and P-15M Squat Eye early-warning (EW) radars, communications antennas, and support vans. Planners initially conceived a cross-border raid, but Schwarzkopf balked, recognizing how a ground incursion into Iraq could get out of hand and derail his plan. So they selected AH-64A Apache gunships led by USAF MH-53J Pave Low pathfinders. The big tan-and-brown Pave Lows were armed and armored; had infrared missile countermeasures; all-weather day–night avionics; terrain-following/terrain-avoidance radar (TF/TA); forward-looking infrared vision (FLIR); and Global Positioning System (GPS) navigation; and a ramp from which crewmen could drop IR chem lights to provide visual cues for the Apache pilots.

Red Team struck "Nevada," the westernmost site, and White Team (with Comer and Cody) hit "California," the easternmost. The sites had to be destroyed precisely at 0238L. "It was incredibly dark," Maj Gen Michael Kingsley recalled, "and even our night vision goggles had trouble amplifying the available light." Flying at 145mph at 50–75ft up desert wadis, the Pave Lows flew to a marshaling point near each target. There, the door gunners and flight engineers dropped the IR lights, and the big helicopters turned south to a holding area.

Hovering over the lights, the Apache teams updated their inertial navigation systems, then, 90 seconds early, moved into firing position, the gunners activating their targeting lasers. At 0237:50L pilot Lt Tom Drew radioed "Party in ten," and at precisely 0238L, a dozen miles apart, the two teams unleashed a barrage of Hellfire missiles, ripples of Hydra-70 flechette rockets, and 4,000 rounds of 30mm chain-gun fire, obliterating the two sites. One Apache had its rotor blades holed by bullets, and at least two missiles were fired at a departing Pave Low. Signals intelligence picked up a frantic call to the an-Nukhayb intercept operations center. Though it ended abruptly, the IOC clearly passed it on, for gunners in Baghdad began firing wildly, continuing for several minutes until their barrels overheated or they exhausted their available ammunition.

Stealth: striking out of the "dark corners"

At approximately the same time, the first wave of dull black F-117As slipped into Iraq. Because of their very low radar cross-section (RCS), F-117As were the only aircraft that could transit Iraq's radar maze to seek out and destroy hardened targets. (Cruise missiles – both the AGM-86C and the TLAM-C/D – could only destroy "soft" targets.) Planners used a computer, "Elvira" (after Cassandra Peterson's vampish character "Elvira, Mistress of the Dark"), backed up and refined by human planners, to map ingress and egress routes. "We walk in the shadows," a F-117A pilot quipped, "and Elvira finds us the dark corners."

The F-117A force even had their own bespoke "bunker buster" weapon: a hardened 2,000lb Paveway laser-guided bomb (LGB), the GBU-27. The stealth fighter could carry two GBU-27s, a highly accurate glide weapon capable of striking within 10ft of an aimpoint. The F-117A defeated SAMs by its minimal radar return. Thus, if a pilot attempted to maneuver against a SAM, he actually risked *increasing* the F-117As' perceived RCS. Since the F-117A had never seen combat beyond a single bomb-run on Rio Hato in Operation *Just Cause*, its pilots – hand-picked and rigorously security-screened – had to trust that Lockheed got the RCS right over a decade of static pole-tests and dynamic flight testing at ranges across the western United States.

The F-117A had forward-looking infrared (FLIR) and downward-looking infrared (DLIR), the latter used for targeting. At 0251L, after arriving undetected over the an-Nukhayb IOC and having carefully placed a laser spot on it, then-Maj Gregory Feest disgorged a GBU-27, watching as the bunker's doors and vents blew out. A trailing F-117A hit a second bunker one minute later. Having just dropped *Desert Storm*'s first bomb and "feeling pretty good about myself," he turned towards his next target, a sector operations center (SOC) in the west.

As Feest flew off, far in the distance, bursting flak and arcing tracer erupted for a second time over Baghdad, punctuated by rocketing SAMs. Its defenders commanded 552 SA-2, -3, -6, -8, and Roland 1/2 SAMs, 1,267 antiaircraft cannon, and 6,100 mobile antiaircraft weapons, and they had made some shrewd assumptions. When EF-111As jammed towards Baghdad, they realized the capital would be attacked. When their radars showed no targets, they realized the attackers were F-117As. When 37th TFW (P) planners requested EF-111

"Party in Ten": Pave Low Leads the Way

In the early hours of January 17, 1991, a dozen Air Force Sikorsky MH-53J Pave Low III and Army McDonnell-Douglas AH-64A Apache helicopters raced low across the Iraqi border north of Ar'ar, Saudi Arabia. It was dangerous, low-level flying on a dark, moonless night, the crews at risk both from any Iraqi military forces they might encounter as well as from simply flying into the ground.

Their mission: blast a hole in Iraq's air defenses by destroying two radar sites before they could detect incoming coalition strike aircraft entering western Iraq. The two radar sites, separated by a dozen miles, had a mix of P-12 Spoon Rest, P-15 Flat Face, and P-15M Squat Eye early warning radars, plus command and communications vans and systems. Time-on-target was set for precisely 0238L, so pin-point navigation and timing was a must. That necessitated having Pave Low pathfinders, with terrain-following/terrain avoidance (TF/TA) radar, forward-looking infrared vision (FLIR) and Global Positioning System (GPS) satellite navigation leading the Apaches to a predetermined geographical reference point near each site.

The helicopters were divided into two teams: Red Team attacked the westernmost site, designated Nevada, and White Team attacked the easternmost site, California. Each team paired two Pave Low pathfinders from the Air Force's 20th Special Operations Squadron (commanded by Lt Col Richard L. Comer), with four Apache gunships from the Army's 1st Battalion, 101st Aviation Regiment (commanded by Lt Col Richard A. "Dick" Cody). Both were "lead-from-the-front" commanders, and they each flew that night.

Thanks to intensive pre-war preparation and rigorous joint training, the attack came off smoothly. In order to reach their targets simultaneously, the two teams crossed the Saudi–Iraq border at slightly different times, the first entering Iraqi airspace at 0212L. White team proceeded due north, Red Team north-northwest. Crews saw some tracers even as they maneuvered around known observation posts. The Pave Lows led the teams to the predetermined reference point, door gunners and flight engineers dropped chem light markers, and the big tan-and-brown helicopters turned south to a holding area. The Apache crews updated their inertial navigation systems, then moved into firing position, 90 seconds earlier than planned.

Perhaps hearing the distant rotors, Iraqi air defenders began turning off the lights at the two sites, but it was too late. The Apache gunners turned on their targeting lasers. At 0237:50L Apache pilot Lt Tom Drew radioed "Party in ten," and at precisely 0238L, a dozen miles apart, the two Apache teams unleashed a welter of carefully aimed Hellfire missiles, then, after moving closer, followed up with ripples of Hydra-70 flechette rockets, and bursts of 30mm chain-gun fire. In three minutes the sites were obliterated, at the price of one Apache having its rotor blades holed by bullets, and at least two SA-7s fired at a Red Team egressing Pave Low, which evaded them.

"It went exactly as planned," Comer recalled on the twentieth anniversary of *Desert Storm*; "The mission was a perfect success. The Iraqis now had no eyes to see with over a large portion of their border and a coalition air armada streamed into the country above our two helicopter formations."

Here White Team's Capt Mike Kingsley's Pave Low, followed by that of Maj Bob Leonik (with Comer as his co-pilot) is shown on the egress, with Chevy Flight's F-15E Strike Eagles from the 336th Tactical Fighter Squadron of the 4th Tactical Fighter Wing passing overhead, inbound to hit fixed Scud launchers at H-2 air base.

A Lockheed F-117A drops its signature GBU-27 Paveway III laser-guided bomb (LGB) over the Utah Test and Training Range (UTTR). Every angle and angular relationship of its carefully faceted body – highlighted here by the sun angle – as well as the leading and trailing edges of all forward and trailing surfaces (see the "sawtooth" weapons bay doors) – reflected the need to minimize frontal and rearward radar return to frustrate radars "dwelling" on it and establishing a track. The F-117A holds the distinction of being the first airplane in aviation history in which aerodynamic shaping took a distant second place to electronic signature shaping during its design phase. (DoD)

support as insurance, Buster Glosson had predicted this would happen. "The EF-111s are going to tip everyone off," Glosson said, "and everybody's going to see barrage fire like they've never seen in their life."

Within that deadly lightshow, six F-117A drivers pressed on to their targets, the first of 39 hit in Baghdad over the war. At 0300L, Capt Marcel Kerdavid dropped a single GBU-27 on Baghdad's 370ft tall al-Karakh telecommunications tower, turning towards al-Taji to drop a second. Maj Jerry Leatherman dropped both his GBU-27s on Baghdad's telephone exchange (dubbed the "AT&T building"), designed with multiple redundant and duplicate floors handling domestic, regional, and international communications. Those "in the know" watched CNN's live feed from Baghdad. Reporter Peter Arnett had just finished "The Iraqis have informed us . . ." when the screen went blank. In the Black Hole, the TACC, and in Checkmate, wild cheers erupted: "It was a wonderful moment," Horner recalled.

At 0305L four other F-117As hit air force headquarters, the al-Taji Sector Operations Center (SOC), the already damaged AT&T building (to ensure it was knocked out), and the Tallil SOC. They then struck other air defense and command, control, and communications targets with their second bombs. At 0306L – not before, as sometimes alleged – the first TLAMs arrived, hitting Ba'ath Party headquarters, the "Republican Palace" at Abu Ghraib (seat of the Saddam regime), and electrical transmission facilities; others followed at 0330L, striking the al-Taji weapons complex and Al Samarra's chemical warfare laboratories.

As he returned across the Saudi border, Feest was "shocked" he had emerged safely. As he and other "Bandits" air-refueled for the long return south to Khamis, he ticked off each callsign. After 30 minutes, he recalled, "I knew we had all made it out." Walk-arounds revealed none had any damage. "We had nothing wrong with any of our aircraft, and nobody had got hit," Feest recalled, "so we were starting to believe in stealth technology." "The F-117A pilots aren't interested in any more EF-111s," Col Tolin, a past commander of the 37th TFW, told Glosson the next morning; "They said the barrage fire was unbelievable."

Confronting Iraq's layered air defenses

Between 0340L and 0420L, the Coalition's fighters and strikers went after the Iraqi air force, with fighter sweeps, airfield strikes, and a "gorilla package" striking Iraq's remaining air defenses and radars. The package, "Poobah's Party," honored Brig Gen Larry "Poobah" Henry. TAC's Gen Bob Russ had detailed Henry to work with Horner's planners. Poobah Henry looked at KARI like a complex watch mechanism, studying where it might have "sprockets" he could disable. He was determined to confuse radar operators into thinking they were looking at massive attack forces by using drones and decoys. That would alarm them so much they would illuminate their radars, revealing their locations for anti-radar missiles.

The SEAD package included A-6, A-7, EA-6B, EF-111A, F-4G and F/A-18 HARM-shooters, decoy-launchers, and jammers, in addition to Tornado ALARM-shooters, other attackers, ADM-141A TALD decoys and BQM-74C Chukar drones, and orbiting EC-130H Compass Call jammers to disrupt Iraqi fighter communications. Radar jamming forced Iraqi radar operators to increase the power of their pulses to "burn through" jamming, thereby greatly increasing their own signature, and, hence, vulnerability to HARM and ALARM missiles. Subsequently, Air Force, Navy, and Marine defense suppression aircraft fired 500 HARMs (averaging one every three minutes) over the first day. Over 200 were fired in the first hours – 118 of them from Wild Weasels – during Poobah's Party. It shattered any remaining coherence in Iraqi air defenses, evident when SIGINT tracked abrupt drops, breaks, and interruptions in Iraqi communications. KARI was effectively dead – and the war was less than two hours old.

But Iraq's stand-alone antiaircraft defenses still sobered all who encountered them. "All I could think," Tornado F.3 pilot Sqn Ldr Paul Brown recalled, "was 'God, are those poor bastards going into that?'" A-7E pilot Cdr John "Lites" Leenhouts saw "overwhelming" flak that "looked like the fireworks display at Disney World multiplied by a hundred." Nearing Tallil (Abu Talib AB), Tornado pilot Flt Lt N.J. Heard was "staggered at the amount and intensity of the fire [and] my mouth went completely dry." Egressing after striking Mudaysis, Wg Cdr Jerry Witts saw "a wall-to-wall incandescent white curtain of light" of "horrendous" flak erupt over another airfield. To Marine A-6E pilot Lt Col Waldo Cummings Jr, "It seemed every Iraqi who could put his finger on a trigger had pressed down and wouldn't let go." Skimming the desert enroute to as-Salman airfield, B-52G aircraft commander Capt John Ritter encountered "tracers galore from multiple points," the fire so bright it tripped a safety relay protecting his Buff's Westinghouse AN/AVQ-22 low-light-level TV (LLLTV) from *sunlight* damage.

Iraq's light antiaircraft, mobile SAMS, and shoulder-fired IR missiles forced caution through war's end. Overall, in the first three days, the Coalition lost 11 (and perhaps 12) aircraft on low-level strikes: 4 RAF Tornado GR.1s, 1 Kuwaiti A-4KU, 1 Italian Tornado IDS, 1 Saudi Tornado IDS, 1 USMC OV-10, 1 USAF F-4G, and 2 USN A-6Es. An F-15E last seen climbing into a loft-bombing attack on a petroleum, oil, and lubricant strike near Basra may have fallen to flak or IR missiles, or simply flown into the ground. As well, over the same period, flak and missiles damaged three B-52Gs, an A-6E, an A-10, an F-111F, and four Jaguar As.

That the Coalition lost aircraft to Iraq's low-altitude defenses surprised neither Chuck Horner, nor Stan Arthur, nor SPEAR's "Carlos" Johnson, each of whom had cautioned against low-level attack, their wisdom hard-learned over North Vietnam. Well before the war, as 9th AF commander, Horner had flown an F-15E familiarization flight, then addressed the 4th TFW's F-15E pilots and WSOs, telling them "When people are shooting at you and you're at low level, you're stupid, you're a target." His remarks hadn't gone over well: the aircrew had stared back at him "like I was from Mars." For them, low-level strike was more than tactical doctrine: it was a sanctified article of faith Church of TAC dogma. Carlos Johnson's SPEAR analysts likewise concluded low level over Iraq was no place to be, but when he briefed their conclusions to Stan Arthur's air wing and squadron commanders in

The RAF's variable-sweep Panavia Tornado GR.1 strike and GR.1A recce crews flew with exemplary courage on dangerous and physically demanding low-altitude strikes against Iraqi airfields and other targets, and undertook deep reconnaissance and Scud hunting. This GR.1 Gulf veteran, ZA374, is now preserved at the National Museum of the US Air Force, thanks to (the late) RAF air attaché and Dhahran Operation *Granby* Tornado force commander Air Commodore Jerry Witts. Note the two large 2,250l (594-US gal.) external gray fuel tanks; originally developed for the all-gray high-altitude Tornado F.3 interceptors patrolling the Iceland–UK Gap. Dubbed "Hindenburgers," they were adapted for the GR.1/1A as they afforded Tornado crews an additional 15 minutes of low-level flying time: seemingly small but crucially important for the missions flown from Saudi Arabia into Iraq by the GR.1 / GR.1A force. (Photo Ken LaRock, DoD)

early December, they reacted exactly as had Horner's airmen. "The sound of wind whistling through teeth could be heard," RADM Samuel Cox recalled three decades later, adding, "The discussion was heated." Like Horner, Stan Arthur preferred leaving tactics up to strike leaders, air crews, and air intelligence officers aboard his carriers. Nevertheless, after the first losses, Arthur sent his air wing and squadron commanders a terse message. "Gentlemen, far be it for me to dictate specific combat tactics [but] one cannot escape the fact that [the] current AAA environment makes low altitude delivery a non-starter."

The Iraq Air Force comes up to fight

Amid the bursting antiaircraft fire and rocketing SAMs, small numbers of MiG-29A, MiG-23ML, Mirage F-1EQ/BQ, and MiG-25PD fighters launched in an uncoordinated (if spirited) effort to confront Coalition attackers. Electronic jamming of Iraqi communications and both ground and airborne radars, coupled with the initial smart bomb and anti-radar missile strikes on GCI sites and air operations centers, left them with at best sporadic communications and cuing, and their own onboard radars operated with only varying success. A 39 Squadron MiG-29A out of Mudaysis approached an ingressing ground-skimming Tornado, the pilot of which warned by his strobing radar-warning receiver, prudently maneuvered leftward away from it. Fortunately, the MiG passed to the right, as the warning strobe faded and ceased.

Stealth pilots were saved by their very low radar signature and dull gray-black finish. An ingressing F-117A pilot FLIR spotted two 73 Squadron MiG-23MLs approaching head-on that passed without detecting him. A 63 Squadron MiG-23ML missed another F-117A, too faint to be detected and tracked by its mediocre NIIR RP-23ML Sapfir (NATO High Lark II) radar.

A dozen Air Force F-15C Eagles and a dozen Navy F-14A/A+ Tomcats flew fighter sweeps and CAPS in the expectation that once the F-117As had shattered KARI's basic structure, air defense commanders would order Iraqi fighters into the air. The Nomads of the 33rd TFW (P) downed three near Mudaysis (Talha AB): the first fell to Capt Jon K. "J.B." Kelk (Pennzoil 63), and the second and third to Capt Robert E. "Cheese" Graeter (Citgo 61). Slightly later, the 1st TFW (P)'s Capt Steven "Tater" Tate (Quaker 11) shot down a fourth outside Abu Ubaida Ibn al-Jarrah (al-Kut-al-Hayy AB). Initially listed as a MiG-29A and three Mirage F-1EQs, the tally appears to have been a 39 Squadron MiG-29A shot down by Kelk; two other 39 Squadron MiG-29A Fulcrums downed by Graeter (the last of which crashed evading him), these two mistaken for F-1EQs because they had Thomson-CSF Remora jamming pods emitting the Mirage's characteristic electronic signature; and a wandering 79 Squadron two-place Mirage F-1BQ, the pilot of which safely ejected after Tate shot him down.

73 Squadron lost a MiG-23ML Flogger and its pilot south of Mudaysis, blamed on an F-15C. But no Coalition pilot claimed a Flogger kill that night, nor over the next week, and it was likely lost to Iraqi "own goal" air-to-air or surface-to-air fratricide. There was an unreported MiG-29A lost, witnessed approaching head-on by four 4th TFW (P) F-15E crews. Skimming the desert at Mach 0.90 (690mph) at 100ft, they saw it pass, break into a diving turn, and then explode, dribbling flaming wreckage across the desert, its pilot having fatally misjudged converting into a stern attack on the third Strike Eagle. This Fulcrum likewise was unclaimed.

As successful as the Eagles were, the Coalition did not escape unscathed. A 96 Squadron MiG-25PD Foxbat flown by Capt Zuhair Dawood scrambled from Qadisiyah (al-Asad AB) to intercept a combined *Kennedy* CVW-3 / *Saratoga* CVW-17 strike package enroute to bomb al-Taqaddum (Tammuz AB). He found and homed in on Modex 403, a VFA-81 F/A-18C off *Saratoga*, the pilot of which, Lt Cdr Michael Scott Speicher, was in a shallow dive, setting up a HARM launch. "Spike" Speicher wasn't even supposed to fly that night, but had insisted, arguing it was what he had trained for over his entire career. Closing from the left rear in a classic pursuit curve, the Iraqi pilot launched a single R-40RD (AA-6 Acrid) missile that disintegrated the Hornet, the only confirmed Iraqi air-to-air victory in the war. Its wreckage fell south of Qadisiyah, and the Navy subsequently declared its courageous pilot as MIA.[1]

Twice that night attackers turned the table on Iraqi fighters. Tornado pilot Sqn Ldr P.K. Bateson, bombing Qadisiyah (al-Asad AB), spotted a taxiing 96 Squadron MiG-25PD Foxbat, adjusting his run so his JP233 bomblets badly damaged it. At as-Salman, bomblets strewn seconds before by a desert-skimming 4300th BW (P) B-52G wrecked another Iraqi jet.

Opening night: an assessment

Opening night determined the future course of the Gulf War, and highlighted the era of routine precision attack. In World War II, hundreds of aircraft would bomb one or two

1   For years, controversy raged over whether he was alive or dead. As an MIA presumed captured, he was promoted to commander and then captain. Acting on a tip, in 2009, USN/USMC special operators discovered his remains, and he was returned home to Florida and interred with military honors.

"I didn't think anything like this could exist": L'Armée de L'Air attacks Ahmad al-Jaber

At 0530L on the morning of January 17, 1991, a dozen SEPECAT Jaguar A strike-fighters of l'Armée de l'Air's 11e Escadre de Chasse departed Al Ahsa air base in Saudi Arabia, off to raid Kuwait's Ahmad Al Jaber airfield. Some carried four Matra-Thomson BLG 66 Belouga parachute-retarded cluster bombs (151 submunitions apiece), but others had a centerline Thomson-CSF ATLIS (Automatic Tracking and Laser Integration System) target designation pod and a single Aérospatiale AS-30L, a superb Mach 1.75 laser-homing missile with a 240kg (528lb) warhead that could penetrate 2m (6.5ft) of reinforced concrete at a range of 10km (6.2 miles). They mounted an ESD Barax electronic jamming pod under the left wing, and a Matra-MBDA Magic 2 air-to-air missile under the right, "just in case" Iraqi fighters appeared to contest the mission.

After refueling from three French Boeing KC-135FR Stratotankers from the 93e Escadre de Ravitaillement, they formed up in two groups of six aircraft, and, protected by USAF McDonnell-Douglas F-4G Wild Weasels and a top cover of USAF General Dynamics F-16C Fighting Falcons, crossed into Kuwaiti airspace. As the F-4Gs targeted Iraqi radars, the Jaguars descended to nearly ground level, each group executing a spirited low-level attack, streaking by some of their targets at less than roof-height, and having to dodge powerlines and towers as they weaved over the field.

While the first wave of six had caught the Iraqis by surprise, the second wave, flying in a formation resembling a flattened triangle and attacking just seconds later, flew into a hornet's nest of heavy fire from 9K32 Strela-2 (NATO SA-7 Grail) IR-homing missiles, ZSU-23-4 Shilka 23mm and ZPU-30-2 30mm rapid-firing light cannon, and various small arms. "I didn't think anything like this could exist," one pilot wrote afterwards, adding, "The intensity of the response coming from the ground was incredible."

The sky erupted in flak and tracer, and smoky trails of SA-7 shoulder-fired missiles crisscrossed the sky. In all, four Jaguars were hit, three seriously, but all returned safely. A small-caliber projectile struck the starboard engine of Jaguar A104 (11-EK), the ninth aircraft to attack, which broke away, streaming a banner of black smoke from the ailing engine. Jaguar A91 (11-YG), the twelfth and last to strike, had an even closer call, taking a direct hit from an SA-7 that blew away much of its right engine, starting an engine fire. Its pilot kept his speed up until the fire blew out, and, accompanied by A104, crossed back into Saudi skies. Both aircraft made an emergency landing at the Saudi naval airbase at al-Jubayl, home to US Marine Harriers and Hornets. Another Jaguar pilot had a very close call from a small-caliber projectile that shattered his canopy, hitting and holing his helmet, but fortunately only slightly wounding him. Dazed but drawing upon reserves of raw courage and consummate skill, he returned safely to Al Ahsa.

The raid proved that French airmen had not lost the courage, élan, and verve their predecessors had shown in multiple wars, however, it offered a sobering lesson as well on the dangers of low-level attack, particularly in the face of threats such as the notorious Shilka and Strela. Like the rest of the Coalition's airmen, after this initial fling at low-altitude attack, subsequent attacks were made from medium altitude. By war's end, French airmen had flown over 2,250 sorties, and without any lost to Iraqi fire – though, as their day-one experience showed, it could have been far, far different.

Opening night: Carrier Air Wing 3 (CVW 3) LTV A-7E Corsair II pilots of VA-72 (center) and VA-46 (left) prepare for launch from the Red Sea carrier USS *John F. Kennedy*. The aircraft in the middle is carrying AGM-88 HARM anti-radar missiles, while the A-7E immediately opposite it on the left is carrying TALD decoys. (DoD)

aimpoints with little expectation of hitting them, tacitly resorting to area-bombing instead, with consequent heavy civilian casualties. The Gulf War was different: weather permitting, a single strike aircraft with one or two crewmen could now drop laser-guided bombs within 10ft (3m) of an aim point, enabling focused destruction of things with human losses limited largely to military personnel at the target: that was the difference in air power over not quite 50 years.

In the early hours of January 17, 1991, 785 attackers (supported by 478 other aircraft) struck approximately 144 targets having a total of 370 individual targeting aimpoints, called DMPIs – "Desired Mean Point of Impact." The strikes were simultaneous, and parallel – that is, multiple formations proceeding to multiple targets falling in multiple categories. They were also nodal, what would later be called "effects-based operations" (EBO) – the notion that it might not be necessary to hit all the targets within a certain category, just some key targets that resulted in disproportionate destruction to a particular target class, for example electrical power distribution.

By the morning after the first night, Coalition aircraft were freely roaming deep into Iraq. "Horner and his planners," Schwarzkopf noted later, "clearly succeeded brilliantly." Britain's de la Billière, judged it "a masterpiece of human planning and computer-controlled aggression, directed with a degree of precision which far surpassed that of any air attack in the past," adding that many "had been faintly skeptical about the claims which the Americans made for [LGBs]. Now we saw that everything they had said was justified."

And so did Iraq's military leadership: in Baghdad, Gen Georges Sada was at air force headquarters when a series of muffled rumbles heralded a "tremendous explosion" leaving the building "full of dust and debris and smoke" and only with "makeshift communications:" a GBU-27 had hit the quarters of the Iraqi air chief, Lt Gen Muzahim Sa'b Hassan Al-Tikriti, who was elsewhere, having mysteriously offered the use of his quarters that night to Sada. At 0500L, Saddam showed up, shocked at the attack, telling Muzahim (now present) to abandon plans to bomb Israel, adding "It's too late now and we have many other things to think about."

Grappling in the Central Blue

On Day One, January 17, the Iraqi Air Force again came up to fight, losing four fighters to USAF, USMC, and USN pilots. Two 6 Squadron MiG-29As fell near al-Taqaddum (Tammuz AB) to 33rd TFW (P) F-15C pilots Capt Chuck "Sly" Magill (a Marine F/A-18C exchange pilot) and Capt "Hoser" Draeger. Then Lt Cdr Mark "MRT" Fox and Lt Nick "Mongo" Mongillo piloting two *Saratoga* VFA-81 F/A-18C Hornets – bound for H-3 (al-Wallid AB) with four 2,000lb Mk-84 bombs apiece – downed two 47 Squadron MiG-21bis Fishbeds closing head-on at Mach 1.2 (814mph, 707kts), making for a Mach 2.1 merge (1,425mph, 1,237kts). Fox and Mongillo then rolled in on H-3, and, diving through heavy flak, "shacked" a hangar, some other buildings, and a fuel storage, before egressing, the only time in history that bomb-loaded fighters have shot down opposing aircraft and continued on to bomb their targets.

On Day Two, January 18, the Iraqi Air Force stood down, save for moving aircraft about. Day Three, on January 19, was a busy one, Eagle pilots of Tabuk's 33rd TFW (P) and Incirlik's *Proven Force* knocked down two 97 Squadron MiG-25PDs, two 39 Squadron MiG-29As, and two 91 Squadron Mirage F-1BQs. The engagements were hard-fought: the Iraqi pilots showed determination, skill, persistence, and tactical finesse, exploiting "Doppler notch" vulnerabilities in the E-3 AWACS' AN/APY-1 search radar and the F-15C's Hughes AN/APG-63 X-band pulse-doppler radar to minimize detection, and attempted to lure the Eagles into "SAMbushes."

By Day 6, January 22, senior Iraqi officers recognized the Coalition had gained total air supremacy. Its planes, they wrote, were "freely present in all regions of Iraq," while their own air force was pinned to its bases. Sixteen Iraqi fighters had been shot down, 14 by F-15Cs and 2 by F-18Cs, while only one Coalition aircraft had fallen to an Iraqi fighter. Then, on Day 7, January 23, the Coalition began bombing Iraq's hardened aircraft shelters (HAS).

On Day 8, January 24, the Iraqi Air Force struck back. The mission, conceived the previous August, was imaginatively planned, reflecting lessons from the Iraq–Iran war, and its exposure to French military aviation practice. It envisioned two nearly 450-mile (725km) strikes from Abu Ubaida (al-Kut-al Hayy AB) against Saudi Arabia's inland Abqaiq pumping station and coastal Ras Tanura oil terminal complex, following a dog-leg course southeast from Abu Ubaida to Amara, then south-southeast, crossing over Basra and then proceeding on to their targets. Sixteen F-1EQs from 81 and 89 Squadrons would fly: two as escorts, and eight tankers carrying centerline Intertechnique refueling pods, to probe-and-drogue "buddy" refuel six strikers. The tankers would refuel the strikers near Basra, conducting the refueling at an altitude of only 50m (165ft). Four Mirages would hit Abqaiq and two Ras Tanura, with 400kg (880lb) HE bombs.

Attacks on the 23rd that destroyed several Mirages and scattered bomblets across the field delayed the mission by a day. The next morning, the Abqaiq group could not manage the refueling. The Ras Tanura package did; after their escorts and tankers peeled off, the two F-1EQ strikers, Maj Ali Hussein and Capt Mohammad Saleem, 89 Squadron's commander and deputy commander, continued on. They flew low and paralleled the Kuwaiti–Saudi coastline, perhaps by chance, though more likely because Iraqi air intelligence knew this exploited a north–south administrative "seam." While Horner's CENTAF oversaw air ops over land, Capt Thomas "Tom" Marfiak, NAVCENT's Antiair Warfare Commander (AAWC) and skipper of the *Bunker Hill* (CG-52), oversaw air ops over the Gulf. Further complicating this were communications incompatibilities between CENTAF and NAVCENT.

Several aircraft detected the Mirages, and a USAF E-3 AWACS voice-warned the fleet and passed position and bearing, then ordered the nearest fighters, four Saudi 13th Fighter Squadron F-15Cs led by Capt Ayed Salah al-Shamrani, to intercept. Also, the USS *Worden* (CG-18) vectored two CVW-8 F-14As from the carrier *Roosevelt* and some CVW-5 F/A-18As off *Midway* (CV-41). But al-Shamrani arrived first. "I just rolled in behind them and shot them down," al-Shamrani stated later, adding, "You know the F-15, nobody can beat it." Both Mirages and their brave pilots fell close to the fleet, within Exocet-range had they been carrying them.

On Day 10 and 11, January 26 and 27, 33rd TFW (P) and 4th TFW (P) Eagles tangled for the first time with Floggers, shooting down three 73 Squadron MiG-23MLs on the 26th and three 49 Squadron MiG-23BN fighter-bombers on the 27th, plus a 79 Squadron Mirage F-1EQ.

A Royal Saudi Air Force McDonnell-Douglas F-15C Eagle approaches the refueling boom of a USAF KC-135 tanker. RSAF–USAF relations were excellent, reflecting long-standing ties. When the first USAF F-15Cs arrived at Dhahran on August 8, RSAF F-15C pilots flew CAP, allowing the Americans to rest until ready, and then took them on local-area orientation flights. There was also the "people factor:" Brig Gen Prince Turki bin Nasser – an F-15C pilot commanding King Abd al-Aziz Air Base at Dhahran and a graduate of the USAF's Air University – formed a strong bond with Gen Horner and Brig Gen John M. McBroom, whose F-15Cs were the first Eagles into Saudi Arabia. Their personal chemistry did much to cement relations between them. (DoD)

Units ●

Attacking Force:

1. 8 McDonnell-Douglas F-15C Eagles from the 27th Tactical Fighter Squadron, 1st Tactical Fighter Wing-Provisional.
2. 2 Grumman-General Dynamics EF-111A Ravens from the 42nd Electronic Combat Squadron, 48th Tactical Fighter Wing-Provisional, for jamming Iraqi radar sites.
3. 8 McDonnell-Douglas F-4G Wild Weasels from the 561st Tactical Fighter Squadron, 35th Tactical Fighter Wing-Provisional, armed with two AGM-88 HARM missiles.
4. 20 General Dynamics F-16C Fighting Falcons from the 17th Tactical Fighter Squadron, 363rd Tactical Fighter Wing (Provisional) to attack As Salman North Air Base.

Supporting Force:

5. 1 Boeing E-3C Sentry AWACS from the 960th Airborne Air Control Squadron, 552nd Airborne Warning and Control Wing-Provisional.
6. 1 Lockheed EC-130E ABCCC of the 7th Airborne Command and Control Squadron, 15th Air Division- Provisional.
7. 1 Boeing RV-135V Rivet Joint from the 1700th Strategic Reconnaissance Squadron-Provisional of the 1700th Strategic Wing-Provisional.
8. 1 Lockheed EC-130H Compass Call of the 41st Electronic Combat Squadron-Provisional, 15th Air Division-Provisional.
9. 10 Boeing KC-135R tankers in two formations of five (one formation for each of two refueling tracks) from the 1702nd Air Refueling Wing (Provisional).

Iraqi Forces

10. Two Sukhoi Su-22M-4 fighter-bombers (NATO Fitter-K) of No. 109 Squadron, Al Shuaiba (Wahda) AB.
11. A dense plethora of SAM and AAA defenses ranging from 23mm through 100mm cannon, and SA-2, -3, -6, -8, Roland 1, and Roland 2 surface to air missiles.

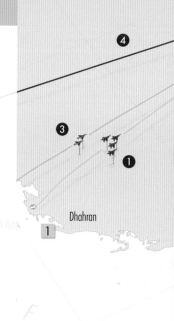

EVENTS

1 Takeoff, 0658L to 0745L: Two Grumman-General Dynamics EF-111A Raven ("Sparkvark") jammers of the 42nd Electronic Combat Squadron (ECS) of the 48th Tactical Fighter Wing (Provisional) (TFW-P) depart Taif AB Saudi Arabia at 0658 Local. Twenty F-16C Fighting Falcons ("Vipers") from the 17th Tactical Fighter Squadron (TFS) of the 363rd TFW-P armed with a mix of cluster bombs and 2,000lb. Mk-84 general purpose bombs follow, depart Al Dhafra, Abu Dhabi (UAE) at 0700L. Eight McDonnell-Douglas F-4G Phantom II "Wild Weasel" radar-killers of the 561st TFS, 35th TFW-P next depart Shaikh Isa AB, Bahrain at 0740. Finally, eight F-15C Eagle air superiority fighters of the 27th TFS, 2st TFW-P depart Dhahran AB at 0745L.

2 Tanker rendezvous and tanking, 0820 to 0830, with Boeing KC-135R tankers occurs on Railroad (West) and Weasel (East) tanker tracks. Each track has one five-aircraft echelon-stacked KC-135R formation. At 0820 the Taif EF-111As arrive at Railroad. The F-4Gs and F-15Cs reach Weasel at 0825L. The F-16Cs arrive at Railroad at 0830.

3 Completion of Refueling, 0850 to 0905. The F-15Cs complete tanking at 0850, the EF-111As at 0853, the F-4Gs at 0855, and the F-16Cs at 0905.

4 Iraqi fighter sorties, 0855 and 0903. Two Iraqi Sukhoi Su-22M-4 Fitters of No. 109 Squadron depart Wahda AB [Al Shuaiba AB] on a "flush" to Iran.

5 Crossing into Iraq, 0857 to 0912. The eight F-15Cs cross the Iraqi border at 0857, taking up two line-abreast 4-ship "Wall of Eagles" formations, one towards As Salman AB, the other towards Abu Talib (Tallil) AB. At 0900 the two EF-111A Ravens cross.

The eight Wild Weasels cross the frontier at 0902. The F-16C strike force crosses into Iraqi airspace from 0912 through 0915, in five four-ship (two element) flights, proceeding in trail.

6 Stand-off mission support, 0900 to 1000. The RC-135V Rivet Joint, E-3A AWACS, EC-130E ABCCC, and EC-130H Compass Call aircraft flying tracks in Saudi airspace provide real-time warning, control, jamming, and intelligence support to the strike package.

7 CAP, Jamming, and SAM-killing forces in place, 0905 to 0911. F-15Cs, F-4Gs, and EF-111As arrive on their Combat Air Patrol (CAP), radar-hunting, and jamming stations. The F-15Cs CAP the As Salman target area and cover other threat air fields beginning at 0905. The EF-111As reach their jamming station at 0908, jamming Iraqi early warning and fire control radars. The F-4G Wild Weasels reach their stations at 0910, four searching for SAM fire-control radars around As Salman, and four confronting SAM radars between Jalibah AB and Abu Talib (Tallil) AB.

8 Iraqi threat radar illuminates, 0916. A mobile Straight Flush SA-6 fire-control radar suddenly radiates, but a Weasel kills it with two AGM-88 HARMs before any SA-6 missiles are launched.

9 Mission accomplished, 0920L to 0923L. Amidst light flak, the F-16Cs attack As Salman AB N, eight with cluster bombs delivered against AAA defenses, and 12 with two 2,000lb Mk 84 general purpose bombs, then withdraw.

10 Force egress, 0930 to 0945. The F-16Cs, back into Saudi airspace at 0930, the EF-111As at 0938L, the F-4Gs at 0940L, and the F-15Cs at 0945.

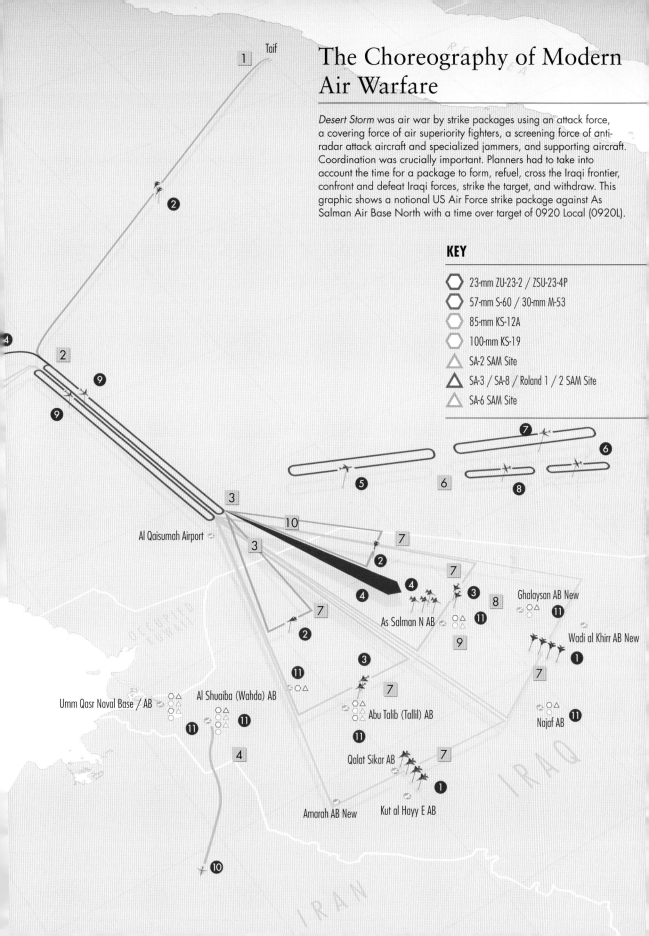

The Choreography of Modern Air Warfare

Desert Storm was air war by strike packages using an attack force, a covering force of air superiority fighters, a screening force of anti-radar attack aircraft and specialized jammers, and supporting aircraft. Coordination was crucially important. Planners had to take into account the time for a package to form, refuel, cross the Iraqi frontier, confront and defeat Iraqi forces, strike the target, and withdraw. This graphic shows a notional US Air Force strike package against As Salman Air Base North with a time over target of 0920 Local (0920L).

KEY

- 23-mm ZU-23-2 / ZSU-23-4P
- 57-mm S-60 / 30-mm M-53
- 85-mm KS-12A
- 100-mm KS-19
- SA-2 SAM Site
- SA-3 / SA-8 / Roland 1 / 2 SAM Site
- SA-6 SAM Site

Taif

Al Qaisumah Airport

As Salman N AB

Ghalaysan AB New

Wadi al Khirr AB New

Umm Qasr Naval Base / AB

Al Shuaiba (Wahda) AB

Abu Talib (Tallil) AB

Najaf AB

Qalat Sikar AB

Amarah AB New

Kut al Hayy E AB

OCCUPIED KUWAIT

IRAQ

IRAN

Iraq had 28 MiG-25 Foxbats, 19 MiG-25PD/PDSs split between two air defense squadrons and nine MiG-25RBs in a reconnaissance squadron. The MiG-25PD/PDS air defense variant combined Mach 2.83 (1,620kt) speed with a good radar and long-range missile, the Vympel R-40RD/TD (NATO AA-6 Acrid), making it a dangerous threat for ingressing Coalition strike forces. (DoD)

More significantly, Day 10 marked the first flush of Iraqi aircraft to Iran. Almost two dozen – including 18 F-1EQs – fled, obeying a directive from Saddam Hussein to his "courageous air falcons." Saddam had long planned the evacuation, sending Izzat Ibrahim al-Douri to Iran two days before the war to secure permission from Iran for the flights. By the 28th, Day 12, over 80 had crossed into Iraq, including two dozen Su-24 Fencers, Iraq's most potent strike warplane. The number, by Iraqi accounting, eventually rose to 137, 131 of which were combat or combat-support aircraft. The table later in this chapter details the disposition of all combat or combat-support aircraft, including combat losses, damaged, flown to Iran or lost en-route, and left in Iraq. After this development, on January 27, Day 11, Schwarzkopf and Horner declared the Coalition had achieved air supremacy – not just air superiority – over Iraq.

By Day 14, January 30, the Iraqi Air Force had lost an additional ten MiG and Mirage fighters, raising the total to 26: 2 MiG-21 Fishbeds, 8 MiG-23 Floggers, 2 MiG-25 Foxbats, 8 MiG-29 Fulcrums, and 6 Mirage F-1EQ/BQs. Of these, 2 fell before an RSAF F-15C, 2 others to USN F/A-18Cs, and 22 more to USAF F-15Cs. As a parting shot, its Foxbat force – down to 15 operational airframes – undertook one final offensive action that day, Operation *Samurrá*, hoping to "humble" the USAF by isolating and destroying a small formation of Eagles by slashing attacks from various directions. But the better-trained Eagle pilots frustrated their adversaries (though, in turn, various failures with their missiles frustrated them, preventing any further Foxbat kills), generating an aerial draw.

After January 30, the Iraqi air force was effectively "on the run," and subsequent engagements were almost always against ones and twos of Iraqi aircraft fleeing to Iran, or otherwise caught unawares. Altogether, Iraq lost an additional 11 airplanes shot down after January 30, and 6 helicopters: 1 Il-76s; 2 MiG-21bis/F-7Bs; 5 Su-20/22s;[2] 2 Su-25s; 1 PC-9; 3 Mi-8s; 1 Mi-24; 1 Bo 105; and 1 Hughes 500. Of these, the USAF scored 16: an F-15E downed a helicopter with a GBU-10 LGB; A-10As gunned down 2 helicopters; and F-15Cs downed 13 including a Pilatus PC-9 trainer (the pilot of which, realizing the hopelessness of his predicament, wisely ejected), and a USN F-14A shot down a fourth helicopter with an AIM-9. Iraqi air-to-air fighter losses over the war totaled 4 Fishbeds, 8 Floggers, 2 Foxbats, 8 Fulcrums, 5 Fitters, 2 Frogfoots, and 6 Mirages, giving the Coalition a 35:1 fighter-versus-fighter victory–loss ratio. Overall, Iraq lost 43 aircraft in air-to-air combat, averaging one per day.

Preventing resurgence: the shelter-busting campaign

The Iraqi air force died not only in the skies, but in its hardened aircraft shelters (HAS). This bunker-blasting effort, which destroyed its last refuge, began on Day 7, January 23, after Horner and Glosson concluded the Iraqi air force was prepared to ride out the war inside its shelters. Having been built to Warsaw Pact standards, they were assumed immune

---

2   Though some records claim these Fitters as Su-7/Su-17/Su-20/Su-22, the operational Fitter fleet was 18 Su-20s (of which 4 were lost) and 78 Su-22M/R/Us (of which 20 were lost); it can be assumed these losses were all Su-20/22M/R/U Fitters.

to Coalition attack. Very quickly, shelter-busting strikes by American, British, Saudi, French, Italian, and other member aircraft dropping laser-guided hardened bombs – particularly 2,000lb. GBU-10Is, GBU-24/BLU-109s, and GBU-27s – disabused the Iraqi leadership of that assumption. Overall, Coalition airmen destroyed 375 of 594 HAS – nearly two-thirds – together with 117 aircraft.

Flown over roughly two weeks, these HAS strikes constituted just 14 percent of all surface-attack strikes in that time period. In fact, however, they constituted a far greater percentage of the strike efforts of individual precision strike aircraft, which could have been applied to other campaign objectives. The 48th TFW (P)'s F-111Fs – the war's most versatile and productive strike aircraft, undertaking varied strategic and tactical missions – flew more than 40 percent of HAS strikes; the 37th TFW (P)'s F-117As executed 18–26 percent of HAS strikes; and the RAF's Tornado GR.1, flew 28 percent of all British precision strikes (using buddy-lasing or its own self-designating TIALD pod) against Iraqi HAS targets. As a result, "By the second week of February, the Iraqi Air Force had reached the point where its sole function was to track its own losses to Coalition attacks," to quote a postwar Institute for Defense Analyses survey of Iraqi communications. And its losses were considerable, then and later.

The following table is Iraq's accounting of the air force's lost, damaged, and interned combat and combat-support aircraft over the war, excluding light executive aircraft, light trainers, and various helicopters. Overall, of a pre-war claimed total of 744 Boeing, Dassault, Ilyushin, Mikoyan, Sukhoi, and Tupolev combat/combat support aircraft of all types (including combat trainer variants), Iraq lost 245 destroyed (35 air-to-air and 210 on the ground), 94 damaged, and 131 flown to Iran, 11 of which were lost en-route, leaving Iran with 120 which it confiscated, thus resulting in 368 of all types (many likely unflyable) remaining in Iraq at war's end. In percentage terms, Coalition air-to-air and air-to-surface sorties cost Saddam's air force not quite a third of its combat/combat-support aircraft. Saddam and the Iraqi Air Force were responsible for sending nearly a fifth to Iran. Overall, then, Iraq lost by combat or its own "flush" to Iran 376 aircraft [245 + 131], slightly over half (50.54 percent) of its pre-war inventory [376/744] of combat/combat-support aircraft, with 368 flyable/derelict/damaged left in Iraq at war's end, slightly less than half (49.46 percent) of its pre-war inventory [368/744].

Armed with Paveway laser-guided bombs, General Dynamics F-111F SN 72-1443 of the 494th TFS taxis out at Taif for another nocturnal mission against Iraq. Flown by the pilots and WSOs of Col Tom Lennon's 48th TFW (P), the F-model Aardvark ruled the night, from strikes against CBW bunkers and missile lagers to airfield HAS strikes and "tank plinking" in the KTO, thanks to its ability to self-designate for LGBs with its AN/AVQ-26 Pave Tack sensor system. (DoD)

Iraqi Combat and Combat-Support Aircraft Lost, Damaged, and Flown to Iran[1]					
Type of aircraft	Prewar total	Number lost	Number damaged	Flown to Iran/ lost enroute	In Iraq at war's end
Boeing 727 ELINT Collector	1	0	0	1	0
Dassault Mirage F-1EQ/BQ	76	23	6	24 / 0	29
Dassault Mirage F-1KU (captured Kuwaiti AF)	8	2	2	0 / 0	6
Ilyushin Il-76MD Adnan 2 "Baghdad" AEW&C[2]	2	1	0	1 / 0	0
Ilyushin Il-76MD	17	2	1	14 / 0	1
Mikoyan MiG-21MF/bis/Chengdu F-7B	236	65	46	0 / 0	171
Mikoyan MiG-23BN/MK/ML/MS/U	127	43	10	12 / 1	72
Mikoyan MiG-25PD/PDS/PU/RB	35	19	6	0 / 0	16
Mikoyan MiG-29A/UB	37	17	4	4 / 0	16
Sukhoi Su-20/Su-22 M-2, -3, -4/R/U	96	24	11	44 / 8	28
Sukhoi Su-24MK	30	5	0	24 / 2	1
Sukhoi Su-25K/UBK	66	31	8	7 / 0	28
Tupolev Tu-16KSR-2-11/Xian B-6D	7	7	0	0 / 0	0
Tupolev Tu-22B/U	6	6	0	0	0
Totals	744	245	94	131 / 11	368

[1] Total number of aircraft flown to Iran was 137, of which 131 were combat or combat-support. The original source contains many blanks, its numbers do not fully tally, and it confuses the MiG-21 with a non-existent "Sukhoi-21." (Corrected here). The Chengdu F-7B is a PRC derivative of the Soviet MiG-21 (NATO Fishbed) and so counted with it. Likewise, the Xian B-6D is the export variant of the Xian H-6D, a Chinese derivative of the Soviet Tu-16 (NATO Badger). The full total of Iraqi aircraft interned in Iran remains uncertain. The 120 shown interned here only refers to the combat types listed, and not to other aircraft such as various business jets (five Falcons and one Jet Star), and non-military transports. "Flown to Iran / Lost Enroute" column accounts for losses enroute (1 MiG-23, 8 Su-20/Su-22, 2 Su-24 destroyed), rather than just listing numbers flown seeking refuge (12 MiG-23s, 44 Su-20/Su-22s, 24 Su-24s). "In Iraq at War's End" column includes those aircraft damaged, but not the ones destroyed. Iran acknowledged only 22 arrivals. Remember, 744 is the total number of these aircraft—not all the aircraft in the Iraqi military.
[2] The Il-76MD Adnan 2 "Baghdad" was an Iraqi Air Force AWACS-like Il-76MD modification with a SDA-G (Iraqi license-built French Thomson-CSF TRS-2105 Tigre G) G-band EW radar in a circular radome strut-mounted above the mid-fuselage. Two were built, with one destroyed in Iraq by Coalition bombing. It was never operational during Desert Shield and Desert Storm. The one which flew to Iran was renamed Simorgh (after a mythical flying beast), given the serial 5-8208, and subsequently modified with a more advanced radar and placed in Iranian service, but was then lost in an accident on 22 September 2009 during an air show; the cause is variously reported as an inflight collision, an engine fire, or separation of the circular radome, which then severed the tail.

As the number of combat-capable Iraqi aircraft declined, so too did the need to transfer personnel, one February 10 (Day 25) log entry reading "There is no need to send any MiG-23 pilots to Sa'ad Air Base [H-2] as there are no functional aircraft." On Day 31, February 16, the air force leadership messaged all bases to "ensure that aircraft are placed outside the fence, one kilometer apart from each other … so that if an aircraft is hit, no other aircraft nearby it will also be damaged." Teams parked aircraft around religious and historical sites (including the Ziggurat at Ur) to discourage Coalition attacks. Ultimately, they even buried partially disassembled ones.

Asked if he was "surprised" the Iraqi Air Force "didn't come up and fight," Horner replied emphatically, "They came up and fought like hell, but we beat them," and USAF Chief Tony McPeak said, "I think they did rather well under the circumstances. They happened to have the second-best air force in the fight. Having the second-best air force is like having the second-best poker hand – it's often the best strategy to fold early."

Per Ardua: Tornado at war

The RAF's Tornado community suffered a quick cluster of losses that drew great media focus, with armchair critics and journalists wrongly implying they were lost delivering JP233 runway-busting munitions. The first fell on January 17, attacking ar Rumaylah. Seen taking 57mm fire as it climbed to loft eight 1,000lb bombs, it was then struck by a missile – either a Roland or 9K33 Osa (NATO SA-8 Gecko). The crew ejected into a brutal captivity. The strike's Mission Report ("MISREP") concluded "Operating by day, at low-level, against heavily defended targets probably cost the Sqn an aircraft and resulted in one crew being held POWs." After the fourth loss, Horner ordered a tactics review, which AVM Bill Wratten (whom Horner considered "an absolute master of his profession") volunteered to oversee.

Wratten's review confirmed the wisdom of moving to medium altitudes, but, back in Whitehall, it rankled a high-ranking RAF officer outside the Operation *Granby* chain of command, causing de la Billière to react in fury "about the authoritarian way he tried to impose his view." De la Billière had great affection for the Tornado crews, having concluded "their bravery was of a quite exceptional order," as did Horner. "No one else even approached the RAF in terms of courage," he said after the war, "They kept saying, 'Give us the tough ones, give us the tough ones, give us the tough ones!'" Back at RAF High Wycombe, Operation *Granby*'s common-sense and forthright joint commander, ACM Paddy Hine, agreed with Wratten, having himself concluded it was time the Tornados went to medium altitude with Weasel and jamming support.

On January 20, RAF Tornados flew their first medium altitude mission, against an-Najaf AB, the MISREP reporting, "All crews agreed that the medium level option, with support felt safer than low-level overflight of defended targets." Though crews had some early difficulties adjusting to the challenges of medium-altitude formation flying in a very highly loaded airplane optimized for low-altitude strike, even so, the switch from low-to-medium altitude "went surprisingly smoothly," as then-Gp Capt Jerry Witts recalled at a 1999 RAF symposium.

But medium altitude brought a marked reduction in accuracy, captured in a MISREP from a night strike on January 31 against seven hangars at Wahda AB (al-Shuaiba AB) by eight Tornados dropping 60 1,000lb bombs. Post-strike analysis indicated only one hangar was hit. "The target would have been ideally suited to PGMs [Precision Guided Munitions]" the MISREP concluded, adding, "and we hope that their arrival in theater will be sooner rather than later."

And it was. On January 23, the RAF ordered Hawker Siddeley Buccaneer S.2B strike aircraft with AN/AVQ-23E Pave Spike laser designators sent from 12 Squadron,

Flown from Muharraq by No. 55 Squadron, the RAF's Hawker Siddeley Victor K.2 refueled RAF and other nations' strike aircraft requiring probe and drogue tankers. The Victor's curvaceous lines, unique swept-crescent wing planform, and sharply swept high-T tail hinted at its past as the fastest early Cold War subsonic strategic bomber, for all Victor K.2s were converted from retired Victor B.2 and B(SR).2 bombers. (DoD)

Off to Iraq: An RAF Muharraq-based 55 Sqn Hawker Siddeley Victor K.2 tanker, with hoses and drogues deployed, is flanked by a Tabuk Detachment 20 Sqn Panavia Tornado GR.1, ZA491 *Snoopy Airways (Nikki)* armed with three 1,000lb laser-guided bombs, and, more distantly, a Muharraq-based Hawker Siddeley Buccaneer S.2B with an AN/AVQ-23E Pave Spike electro-optical laser designation pod to "buddy lase" for the Tornado. (GW-41 AHB-RAF MoD © Crown copyright 1991)

208 Squadron, and from 237 OCU to the Gulf. The first six of an eventual dozen arrived at Muharraq at the end of January and flew their first lasing mission on February 2. That day, capped by four F-15Cs, two Bucs led two Tornados carrying three 1,000lb LGBs apiece in an attack on the as-Samawah highway bridge across the Euphrates. The first Buc flew a teardrop-shaped pattern around the bridge to keep the spot on the DMPI for the first pair of Tornados, the first bomb of which hit squarely on an unfortunate lorry that unwittingly drove under the laser spot just as the bomb arrived. The following Tornados precisely delivered their bombs as well. The strike marked Tornado's rebirth as a highly successful bridge-buster that took down a number of bridges over the Euphrates and Tigris rivers (including multiple ones at the same location, as with as-Samawah, which had three), including bridges at al Madinah (outside al Qurnah), an Nasiriyah, al Falluja, and al Kut. Tornados working with Buccaneers bombed many other targets, all these attacks executed by day as, being a "first-generation" targeting laser, Pave Spike could not "see" in the dark.

In February the Tornado force received two pre-production Ferranti-GEC Marconi-BAe TIALD (Thermal Imaging Airborne Laser Designator) self-designating targeting pods – crews dubbed them "Tracy" and "Sandra" – that could designate both day and night, bringing Tornado fully into its own. TIALD made a tremendous difference, then-AVM Ian Macfadyen quite rightly hailing it as "one of the success stories of this campaign." TIALD's first strike came on February 10, a HAS-busting attack against H-3 (al-Wallid AB); by war's end, TIALD-cued GR.1s had scored 229 hits on 95 sorties, a third of which were at night. On February 13, the Tornado force switched completely to TIALD from Pave Spike, which had an additional "force multiplier" benefit in that it freed the Buccaneer force – now numbering a dozen aircraft – to become strikers themselves, self-designating for their own bombs.

The Iraqi SAM threat: suppressed but not eliminated

Medium altitude, of course, did not confer immunity, and by chance or error, aircraft could still be lost. Four Coalition aircraft flying at medium altitude, two F-16Cs, an F-15E, and an F-14A+, fell to SAMs over January 19–20. Of their six crew, the two F-16C pilots were captured virtually immediately; the F-15E crew had a chance, but rescuers had difficulties locating them. The F-14A+, Slate 46 from VF-103 off *Saratoga*, fell to an unseen SA-2 that climbed through low cloud and blew up before the crew could react. The RIO quickly fell prisoner, but a courageous and tenacious 20th SOS (Special Operations Squadron) MH-53J Pave Low crew commanded by Capt Tom Trask, Moccasin 05, rescued the pilot, Lt Devon Jones. Assisting were various Air Force and naval aircraft, particularly two A-10As flown by Capt Paul Johnson and Lt Randy Goff, Sandy 57 and 58, that strafed two trucks (one with a radio direction-finding antenna), which raced towards the pilot as he desperately ran for the helicopter.

Most disturbing was the Day 3 loss of two F-16Cs from Package Q, a 78-aircraft strike – the war's largest – against Baghdad. A huge and unwieldy strike package, weather-disrupted refuelings, an ill-considered splitting of the screening force, poor mission coordination, a change in attack approach, mixed clouds in the target area, and limited on-station Wild Weasel fuel endurance led to last-to-arrive (and hence unprotected) F-16Cs encountering a firestorm of accurate radar-directed KS-19 100mm flak and radar-guided SAMs. Pilots estimated 20 SAMs were simultaneously in flight, disrupting their attack and forcing some to jettison their bombs and external fuel tanks. One fortunate pilot evaded six, but two others were shot down and taken prisoner. A third F-16C nearly crashed from fuel starvation, saved only by the timely arrival of a plucky Kansas Air Guard KC-135E crew that crossed into Iraqi airspace to refuel it. The episode left Glosson so angry he couldn't speak, "livid" at what he considered fundamental and multiple errors of judgment. Adding to his bitterness, none of the "dumb" bombs dropped by the F-16Cs actually hit their primary target, the Tuwaitha nuclear research facility.

Nor was the United States alone in taking losses: on February 14 the RAF suffered a sixth and final Tornado loss, the last attacker of a formation of eight Tornados and four Buccaneers striking hardened aircraft shelters at al Taqaddum (Tammuz AB) hit by one and possibly two SA-2s, despite the presence of four F-4G Wild Weasels and two EF-111A jammers. The pilot ejected and was taken prisoner, but his navigator, sadly, was killed.

Targeting Iraq's power infrastructure and forces

From opening night onwards, Iraq's unified national electrical grid, fed by approximately 25 generator plants and modulated by over 140 transformer stations, was shattered by nodal TLAM, AGM-86C, A-6E, A-7E, B-52G, F-16C, F/A-18A/C, F-111Es (but not F-111Fs), and RAF Tornado GR.1 attacks on nine key power generation stations (and five others of lesser importance). Virtually immediately, lights went out as evident on satellite imaging of Baghdad at night. Over the first two days, available power plummeted from roughly 9.5 to 4.5GW, declining further to 2GW by the end of the first week. In early February other strikes reduced it to a little over 1GW. There it stayed, with military facilities and headquarters relying upon emergency generators, when available.

The Coalition attacked 16 of 20 oil refineries, reducing Iraq's petroleum refining capacity – three million barrels per day at the beginning of the war – by approximately 35 percent over

Fairchild A-10A Thunderbolt II flown by Capt Paul Johnson, "Sandy 57," who, with wingman 1st Lt Randy Goff, undertook what became an 8-hour combat search and rescue (CSAR) culminating in them attacking and driving off Iraqi forces attempting to seize Slate 46 Alpha as he was awaiting rescue by AFSOC MH-53J Pave Low III "Moccasin 05." For his leadership, aggressiveness, and courage shown that day, Johnson was awarded the Air Force Cross; his aircraft is now in the National Museum of the USAF. (DoD)

OPPOSITE
In one of the war's most remarkable photographs, "Slate 46 Alpha," USN Tomcat pilot Lt Devon Jones, races towards a USAF Air Commando pararescue jumper ("PJ") while the gunner of "Moccasin 05," an MH-53J Pave Low III commanded by Capt Tom Trask, watches for Iraqi forces racing in two trucks toward the landing site. (DoD)

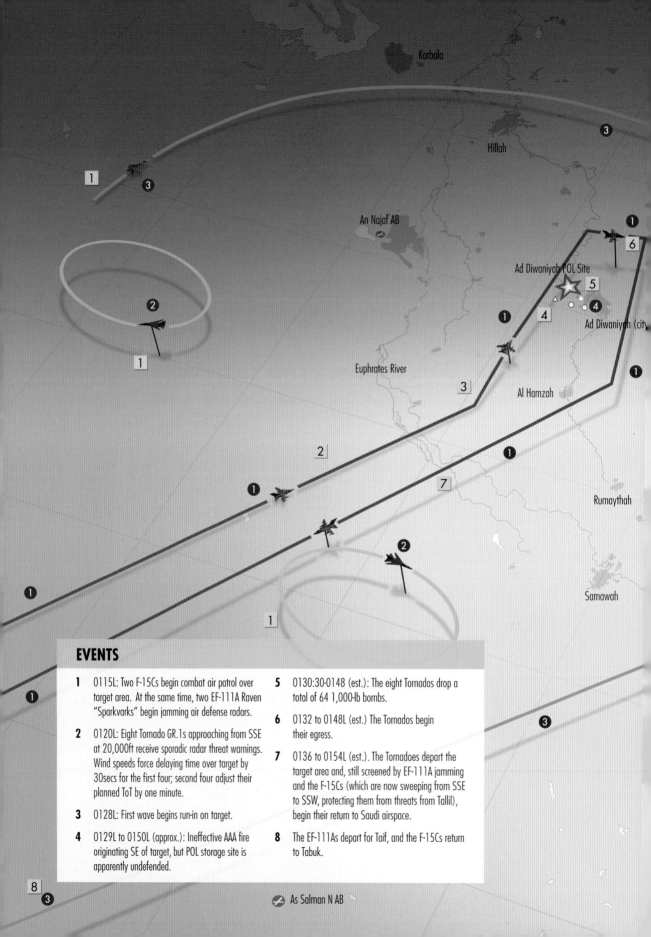

EVENTS

1 0115L: Two F-15Cs begin combat air patrol over target area. At the same time, two EF-111A Raven "Sparkvarks" begin jamming air defense radars.

2 0120L: Eight Tornado GR.1s approaching from SSE at 20,000ft receive sporadic radar threat warnings. Wind speeds force delaying time over target by 30secs for the first four; second four adjust their planned ToT by one minute.

3 0128L: First wave begins run-in on target.

4 0129L to 0150L (approx.): Ineffective AAA fire originating SE of target, but POL storage site is apparently undefended.

5 0130:30-0148 (est.): The eight Tornados drop a total of 64 1,000-lb bombs.

6 0132 to 0148L (est.) The Tornados begin their egress.

7 0136 to 0154L (est.). The Tornadoes depart the target area and, still screened by EF-111A jamming and the F-15Cs (which are now sweeping from SSE to SSW, protecting them from threats from Tallil), begin their return to Saudi airspace.

8 The EF-111As depart for Taif, and the F-15Cs return to Tabuk.

Tornado strike against the Ad Diwaniya petroleum storage site, 29 January 1991

On the night of January 29–30, eight RAF Tornadoes bombed the Ad Diwaniya Petroleum Products Storage Site, consisting of six large storage tanks, eight smaller storage tanks, and various support buildings, within a 900ft x 1,500ft rectangle. Each aircraft carried eight 1,000-lb unguided bombs to be dropped from 20,000ft. The Tornados attacked in two four-aircraft streams, 20secs apart, with 500ft lateral separation between aircraft. Seven bombed successfully; the eighth experienced avionics failure, dropping its bombs 0.5nm short.

Tigris River

An Numaniyah AB

3

Obeida bin al Jarrah (Al Kut) AB

KEY

◇ 23-mm ZU-23-2 / ZSU-23-4P

⬡ 57-mm S-60 / 30-mm M-53

⬠ 85-mm KS-12A

△ SA-3 / SA-8 / Roland 1 / 2 SAM Site

Tigris River

Shatt al Gharraf River/Canal

Kut al Hayy E AB

Qalat Sikar AB

3

7

Units ●

Attacking Force:
1. 8 Royal Air Force Panavia Tornado GR.1 strike aircraft, each armed with eight 1,000-lb dumb bombs, from the Muharraq Tornado Wing.

Supporting Force:
2. 2 Grumman-General Dynamics EF-111A Ravens from the 42nd Electronic Combat Squadron, 48th Tactical Fighter Wing, for jamming Iraqi EW and SAM radar sites and mobile missile radars.
3. 2 McDonnell-Douglas F-15C Eagles from the 58th Tactical Fighter Squadron, 33rd Tactical Fighter Wing (Provisional) for target combat air patrol (TARCAP).

Iraqi Forces:
4. SAM and AAA defenses ranging from 23mm through 100mm cannon, and SA-2, -3, -6, -8, Roland 1, and Roland 2 surface-to-air missiles.

Euphrates River

An Nasiriyah

Abu Talib (Tallil) AB

Tigris River

the first week, dropping by Day 26, February 11, to just 20 percent, and then plunging by Day 34, February 19, to less than seven percent – roughly 195,000 barrels per day. However, attempts to inflict supply denial by targeting oil storage facilities were less than satisfactory, because many Iraqi units (including the Iraqi Air Force) already had what they needed; Iraq's deployed forces were pinned in place by air attack and could not readily (even if they wanted to) move or fly without drawing an air strike upon them; and, being the Middle East, oil was effectively ubiquitous, plentiful virtually everywhere.

Within the first week, Coalition air attacks against Iraqi forces were already alarming Iraqi commanders. One Republican Guard brigade commander, Ra'ad al-Hamdani, reported he had "lost many of [his] officers and soldiers in spite of [his] attempts to decrease the effects of the air bombing as much as possible by having one third of [his] force change positions every day." On Day 5, January 21, Saddam ordered his military to conserve ammunition. The next day he ordered government offices to disassemble and hide equipment, to be uncovered and reassembled once fighting ended.

Ironically, as Saddam grew more concerned about the toll precision air power was taking on Iraq's military infrastructure and its forces, the Coalition's F-15E and F-111F forces causing that destruction were siphoned off to hunt Al-Husseins and attack Iraqi forces in Kuwait (discussed subsequently). To make up for their departure, a further six F-117As arrived from Tonopah, increasing the F-117A force at Khamis to 42. Thus bolstered, the 37th TFW (P) began flying up to three missions per night, including using F-117As as corridor-sweepers for B-52 strikes, the stealth fighters targeting SAM sites that might endanger the big Buffs. The synergy between the EF-111As, EA-6Bs, F-4Gs, F-117As, and the anything-but-stealthy Buff enabled the big bombers to strike the al-Taji weapons development and logistics complex, so vast that it justified broad pattern-bombing to destroy the great number of individual buildings. Between February 10 and 27, 68 B-52G sorties struck al-Taji, dropping almost 3,000 bombs (over 1,100 tons) and inflicting "widespread and severe" damage. On one of these strikes, a 4300th BW (P) B-52G suffered a non-combat inflight emergency, crashing into the Indian Ocean just short of Diego Garcia, killing three of its six crew, the only B-52G loss of the war.

In a week's attacks ending February 14, airmen (the USAF reported) "struck 24 airfields; numerous chemical warfare bunkers; 11 chemical research, production, and development targets; 16 oil targets (including 10 storage facilities); and 53 separate communications targets." Over two nights – February 11/12, and 12/13 – F-117As struck various leadership targets, including Iraq's intelligence service, internal control and security organizations, Ba'ath Party headquarters, the Defense Ministry, bridges crossing the Tigris carrying fiberoptic cables, and various bunkers. The RAF's GR.1/GR.1A Tornado force was likewise active, undertaking HAS strikes on 11 Iraqi airfields, and hitting other targets as well. On February 13, Tornado crews flew 41 sorties including 8 interdiction, 16 counter-air, and 4 recce, protected by F-15C top-cover; EA-6B and EF-111A jamming; and F-4G, F/A-18, and Tornado radar-killers. Over February 15–27, F-117As F-111E/Fs, and RAF GR.1s, hit 17 airfields, security organizations, Ba'ath Party headquarters (again), Saddam's surviving residences, 17 nuclear and chemical targets, the Alteena nuclear research center, the al Musayyib missile development and production complex, 14 C³ facilities, over 30 military support facilities, 13 highway bridges, and numerous mobile Al-Hussein sites.

Finally, at war's end, two F-111Fs dropped a newly developed bomb, the GBU-28, against the Al Taji Command Leadership Bunker Number 2. The deep-penetration GBU-28, developed at Eglin AFB's weapons laboratory in just 17 days and test-dropped over the Tonopah Test Range in Nevada, weighed 4,700lb and had a body tube machined from surplus 8in howitzer barrels. Engineers rushed two by C-141B from Eglin to the 48th TFW (P), their casings still hot from the 630lb of molten Tritonal explosive mix inside. They were still warm when up-loaded onto two F-111Fs, Cardinal 7-1 and 7-2, which, for balance, carried a Mk-84 bomb under their opposite wing. Just hours before the cease-fire, the two dropped their GBU-28s; one missed but the second hit, a gout of flame and smoke bursting out of the bunker's vents and entrances, grimly signaling that the mission – and the bomb – were both successes.

Weather

Desert Storm's air campaign included its share of Clausewitzian "fog and friction" issues that challenged pre-war assumptions, the sequenced priorities of the campaign, and the course of combat operations. The first of these – quite literally fog in some cases – was weather. Weather over Iraq and Kuwait during *Desert Storm* approximated rainy Europe and was the worst of the previous 14 years. It was so bad that it delayed completing the first three phases of the air campaign plan, so that G-Day – the ground invasion into Iraq and Kuwait – was pushed off by over a week. Cloud cover at 10,000ft (3,050m) exceeded 25 percent for nearly three-quarters of the war, 31 out of 43 days; exceeded 50 percent for nearly half the war, 21 days; and exceeded 75 percent for nearly a quarter of the war, 10 days. Accompanying it were violent and gusting winds, pronounced air turbulence, and drenching rains, together with dense low-altitude fogs.

Weather thus impacted all flight operations, from joining formations, refueling, combat, returning to base, and landing, forcing changes in combat planning: for example, 29 changes to the ATO on Day 2, 47 on Day 3, 109 on Day 4, and 395 on Day 5. Dense clouds obscuring the ground masked SAMs popping through the vaporous clag and destroying aircraft before their pilots could counter them. As well, they seriously impacted targeting, for the Coalition's rules of engagement (RoE) demanded positive target identification before weapons release. Weather particularly constrained the use of laser-guided bombs, the only effective weapon against "must-kill" targets, including hardened aircraft shelters (HAS), WMD storage sites, and Iraqi armour and artillery. Of all Coalition precision attackers, F-117As were most affected, both because their laser designator "spot" needed clear skies to be seen, and because F-117A RoE were exacting about ensuring a clearly visible target, since most were in the midst of densely populated urban areas. On February 25, for example, bad weather forced cancellation of all F-117A strikes.

The battle against the Scuds

Shortly before 1100L on January 17, Saddam Hussein sent a note to Lt Gen Hazem Abd al-Razzaq al-Ayyubi, commander of Iraq's Surface-to-Surface Missiles Directorate: "Begin, with Allah's blessing, striking targets inside the criminal Zionist entity [e.g. Israel-ed.] with the heaviest fire possible." Al-Ayyubi relayed Saddam's order to the 224th Missile Brigade in the H-2/H-3 western launch box. Early in the pre-dawn of January 18, they fired eight Al-Husseins at Israel. Another, rising from an eastern launch box between Mutla Ridge and Safwan, arced towards Dhahran, being intercepted by two Raytheon MIM-104C Patriot PAC-2 SAMs fired by the Army's 11th Air Defense Artillery Brigade, the first "in-anger" missile interception. Launched from MAZ-543 (9P117 Uragan) self-contained transporter-erector-launchers (TEL) or the truck-towed al-Waleed mobile erector launcher (MEL), Al-Husseins (invariably called "Scuds"), proved an extraordinarily disruptive wild card of immense strategic significance.

They seriously disrupted the Coalition air campaign: at one point, fully a third of all Coalition daylight sorties were being diverted to the hunt for Scuds, which drew upon space-based surveillance, warning, cuing, and communication; precision attack F-111F, F-15E, A-6E TRAM/MSIP, and GR.1 with TIALD or Buccaneer buddy-lasing; fighter-bombers and attack aircraft like the F-16Cs, F/A-18A/C, A-7E, A-10As, and the Jaguar GR.1A; B-52Gs;

OPPOSITE SCUD INTERCEPTION BY PATRIOT MISSILE

The Soviet R-17 (NATO SS-1C Scud-B) was Iraq's first ballistic missile, and inspired two longer-range indigenous derivatives, the (left) Al-Hussein (also spelled Al-Husayn and Al-Hussain) and the (right) Al-Abbas. The Al-Abbas was a failure, but by the Gulf War, Iraq had approximately 600 Scuds and Al-Husseins including 25 with botulinum, anthrax, and aflatoxin warheads, operated by the Surface-to-Surface Missiles Directorate (SSMD), under Lt Gen Hazem Abd al Razzaq al Ayyubi. The SSMD had two missile brigades, oversaw five missile complexes and 28 fixed launchers around H-1, H-2, and H-3 airfields in western Iraq, and possessed approximately 30 mobile transporter-erector-launchers (TELs) and mobile erector-launchers (MELs). (DoD)

ISR systems like the Lockheed TR-1A ASARS, GR.1A Tornado, and Boeing E-8A J-STARS; and special forces including Britain's Special Air Service (SAS) and Special Boat Service (SBS), Delta Force, and USAF Special Tactics and Combat Controllers, supported by MH-47E, MH-53J, MH-60K, Chinook HC.1, and (briefly) AC-130H aircraft.

The stakes in the Scud hunt were the unity of the Coalition. Saddam banked that the Israelis, long-known for striking back at any attacker, would not stay out of the war. If they came in, he could play the "Zionist enemy" card to split off the Arab members of the Coalition. Intensive diplomatic efforts and immediate deployment of two Patriot PAC-2 missile batteries kept Israel out of the war, despite Saddam's missiles inflicting sporadic damage and casualties.

Altogether, from January 17 through war's end, Iraq missile troops launched 42 Al-Husseins that re-entered over Israel, another 48 that reached Saudi Arabia, and three were fired at Bahrain. (A US Space Command DSP satellite detected 97 launch flares, suggesting four additional Al-Husseins were launched but blew up or fell back to earth during boost-phase.) Patriot AN/MPQ-53 radars assessed 47 of the 93 as threats, firing 158 Patriot PAC-2s against them, a missile so new that only three existed when the Gulf crisis began.

Thanks to early warning and sheltering, the combined death toll from Al-Husseins for both Israel and Saudi Arabia was 42 killed and approximately 450 wounded. Over the length of the war, Al-Hussein hits accounted for 10,750 damaged and destroyed buildings, an average per missile hit of 224. Thirty years on, debates still rage about the relative effectiveness of Patriot. But senior officials who lived under the threat are uniform in its praise. "Patriot was a success, but it wasn't perfect," Israeli Defense Forces' Gen Uri Ram remarked after the war, "Patriot was of enormous strategic significance and helped save lives in Israel from Scud attacks."

Asked his views, Saudi Arabia's Prince Bandar Bin Sultan Bin Abdulaziz said, "I was there and the most beautiful sight in the world that I have ever seen in my life was that Patriot streaking across the capital of Saudi Arabia hitting those Scuds." In 1994, Gp Capt Andrew P.N. Lambert noted, "The effectiveness of [Patriot] is almost entirely irrelevant; both the Saudis and the Israelis believed in them and their deployment steeled frayed nerves – stress was then reduced." Similarly, HRH Lt Gen Khaled bin Sultan wrote after the war, "Just as the Scud was a weapon of terror, so the Patriot proved to be a weapon of comfort."

Overall, the air campaign against Saddam's missiles was frustrating. AC-130Hs were quickly withdrawn after very close calls with MiGs, dense AAA, and SAMs. While aircrew attacked many vehicles and saw many secondary explosions, they were uncertain as to whether they were hitting TELs and MELs and other support vehicles. And there were decoys: al-Ayyubi formed three "brigades" deploying obsolete equipment and high-fidelity decoys to mask the two actual brigades undertaking the attacks: some strikes must have hit these. In a number of cases, fortuitously, SOF forces spotted vehicles and then worked with on-call aircraft in joint attacks, one F-15E squadron commander crediting SAS teams with finding a third of the TELs and MELs his squadron claimed destroyed. On February 26, USAF A-10As, called by an SOF team in western Iraq, spotted at least 20 Al-Husseins east of al Qa'im, apparently husbanded for a final launch against Israel. In a series of attacks, joined by Navy F/A-18A/Cs, all were destroyed.

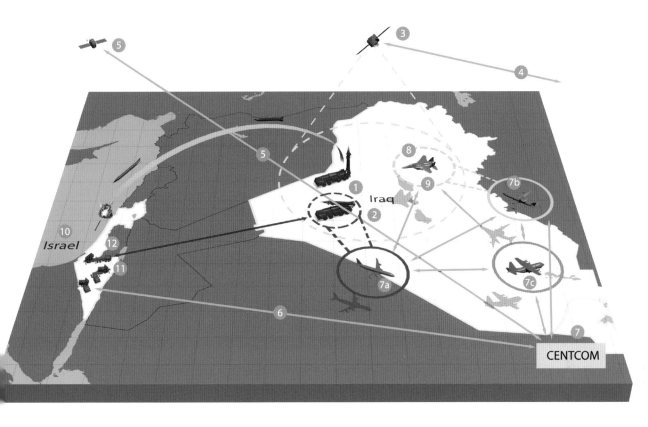

1 An Iraqi MAZ-543 (9P117 Uragan) has deployed to a pre-surveyed launch position at the H-3 Highway Strip.

2 The missile is swiftly erected and launched, and the TEL crew then race to get back under cover.

3 The launch flare is seen by the infrared sensors of an orbiting Defense Support Program (DSP) early warning satellite in geosynchronous earth orbit (GSO).

4 The DSP satellite transmits a launch warning to a US Air Force Space Command ground station at Woomera, Australia. It is then passed to a Defense Satellite Communications System (DSCS) satellite in GSO over the Pacific, which transmits the warning to the Buckley ANG Base in Colorado. Buckley then passes it to US Space Command's Missile Warning Center, the Air Force Space Operations Center, and the Space Command Center, Cheyenne Mountain, Colorado.

5 After determining the likely impact point, the warning and estimated impact point are then sent from Cheyenne Mountain via a DSCS satellite in GSO over the Atlantic to CENTCOM.

6 As soon as it receives the warning, CENTCOM passes it to Israeli air defense authorities who manage engagement control, and thence to a US Army Patriot battery near Tel Aviv.

7 CENTCOM also sends it to three specialized command and control airplanes flying over Saudi Arabia just south of the Iraqi border: (**7a**) A Boeing E-8A J-STARS ground traffic surveillance airplane (**7b**) A Boeing E-3C Sentry AWACS airspace warning and control aircraft, and (**7c**) A Lockheed EC-130E ABCCC battlespace command and control aircraft.

8 These three now oversee a TEL-hunt, sharing information (green arrows) and coordinating with airborne F-15Es (inside the dotted light blue ellipse) which may have already seen the missile launch from a distance and begun racing towards the launch area.

9 The F-15Es (and US/UK special forces) try to locate the retreating Iraqi MAZ-543 TEL and destroy it before it gets under cover. Hunting "shoot and scoot" TELs proved frustratingly difficult, a challenge made harder still by Iraq's use of high-fidelity TEL decoys.

10 In Tel Aviv, the Patriot battery's AN/MSQ-104 Engagement Control Station (ECS) receives the launch and projected impact warning approximately five minutes after the DSP first detected the launch. The battery now has two minutes before impact to acquire the missile with its AN/MPQ-53 narrow-beam radar, and launch Raytheon MIM-104C PAC-2 missiles.

11 Based on previous cuing, the AN/MPQ-53 radar begins scanning the portion of the sky through which the Scud is expected to fly. Having located the target, it then refines its search to both validate that the Patriot battery is tracking the correct target and establish a narrow "range gate", enabling the most accurate firing of Patriots against it.

12 When the ECS's Weapons Control Computer (WCC) reaches its optimum firing solution, the Patriots are launched.

The shocking power of an unengaged Scud or Al Hussain to cause widespread destruction, injury, and death was demonstrated on February 25, 1991, when a missile hit a warehouse being used as quarters by a reserve US Army logistical support group, the 475th Quartermaster Group (Provisional). As many as 28 soldiers perished, and another 97 were wounded, these casualties constituting 36 percent of all US Army killed by enemy action in the war, and 34 percent of all US Army wounded in the war. (DoD)

The most hidden war was waged by British and American special forces across the convoluted wadis and hard lava crusts of western Iraq, amid miserable weather and nights so cold that diesel fuel froze. SAS and SBS teams crossed into Iraq from January 20, supported by Chinook HC.1s of RAF 7 Squadron's Special Forces Flight. The United States first inserted the Army's Delta Force on February 6, using USAF MH-53J Pave Low IIIs from the 20th SOS (since the Army's MH-47s lacked countermeasures to defeat IR missiles), air-refueled by 8th SOS Lockheed MC-130 tankers, and MH-60s of the Army's 160th Special Operations Aviation Regiment (160th SOAR). It was war by night: the air-supported SOF teams lying low and road-watching during the day and Scud hunting at night, punctuated by no-quarter fights with commandos from Unit 999 (a special security battalion from the General Military Intelligence Directorate, GMID). These sometimes necessitated emergency extractions, one of which led to the Gulf War's most unique air-to-air victory. On February 14, an SOF team called for help. AWACS directed Packard 41, a 4th TFW(P) F-15E crewed by Capts Tim Bennett (pilot) and Dan Bakke (WSO) armed with 2,000lb GBU-10 LGBs, to assist. They found five Mil Mi-24 (NATO Hind) troop-carrying gunships low over the desert and moving eastwards, occasionally dropping off soldiers and clearly trying to "herd" the SOF team. They lasered the lead Hind, dropping a GBU-10 that hit it in flight, blowing it to pieces; the others fled, and the SOF team was then extracted.

Despite the counter-missile effort, there were close calls and tragic hits. At 0207L on February 16, an unengaged al-Hussein (the local Patriot battery was down for maintenance) struck Al Jubayl harbor, landing just yards from eight vessels, including a Polish hospital ship and the amphibious assault carrier *Tarawa* (LHA 1). Fortunately, its warhead did not explode: stacked on the pier were 5,000 tons of artillery shells and bombs. Shrapnel or a direct hit could have triggered a 5KT blast, inflicting thousands of casualties. (The Halifax, Nova Scotia munitions ship disaster of 1917 that killed or injured 10,000 people and devastated that port was approximately 3KT.)

The Coalition's luck ran out on February 25, when, at 2023L, an unengaged Scud launched from southern Iraq struck a Dhahran warehouse, which had been converted into a temporary barracks, and exploded, killing 28 US Army soldiers and wounding another 97. Tragically, a Patriot software quirk that generated cumulative errors the longer a Patriot radar operated had led to a steady drift in the radar's range gate calculation that effectively caused the engagement radar to look in the wrong place for the incoming missile. Therefore, by not "seeing" an Al-Hussein, it did not reach a firing solution – and thereby 125 American service personnel died or were wounded.

Clash of arms at al-Khafji: Saddam's calculated lashing-out

On the evening of January 29, the 5th Mechanized Division of the Iraqi III Corps crossed into Saudi Arabia on a mission to lock Coalition forces in a punishing land battle that would prematurely trip the ground war, frustrating Schwarzkopf's plans for an orderly, progressive campaign on his, not Saddam's, schedule. The incursion had been predicted in an August 1990 point paper by the author (then working with the Secretary of the Air Force's Staff Group, SAF/OSX) for Col John Warden entitled "Expectations of Success of Iraqi Forces During a Coastal Drive from Kuwait in Light of Historical Experience." It noted that a short thrust down the coast on the order of 20–30km (12.5–18.5 miles) might succeed unless promptly countered, but that "the presence of even lightly equipped antitank forces on the ground, coupled with persistent air attack from both fixed-and-rotary-wing assets, would deny the enemy freedom of maneuver, result in bottlenecks, result in severe attrition, and shatter confidence and morale of the Iraqi armored forces in their ability to continue their attack." And indeed, that is precisely what occurred.

The incursion triggered a three-day battle in which the Iraqi forces – the 5th Mechanized Division, supported by the 3rd Armoured Division, and including off-shore Iraqi naval elements – were thoroughly shattered by Coalition air attack coupled with resolute resistance on the ground by Saudi and Qatari troops and US Marines. Marine strikes against the three columns by AH-1W attack helicopters and AV-8B Harriers began almost immediately, cued by venerable OV-10 spotters and assisted by AAI RQ-2A

The Anglo-American McDonnell-Douglas AV-8B Harrier II vectored-thrust light strike fighter formed an important part of Marine air power in the Gulf War. Harriers undertook a number of attacks across the KTO, demonstrating the versatility and utility of the type, but also took losses from low altitude air defenses, particularly IR-guided missiles. (DoD)

Pioneer "drones" flying into Iraqi airspace and spotting forces on the border, but, fortunately, no heavy massing of Republican Guard tanks. The first CENTAF aircraft struck Iraqi forces at 2300L. Thereafter, an AC-130 gunship, two F-15Es, two F-16Cs, and four A-10s joined Marine air already in action, blasting Iraqi armored and mechanized forces with a mix of cannon fire, Maverick missiles, smart bombs, and cluster munitions. By the next morning, January 30, the westernmost Iraqi thrust had been halted. The middle column advanced due south from the al-Wafrah oil field, but, again, joint service air attacks and determined Marine resistance shattered its advance. The third column, coming down the coast road, overran al-Khafji, a small port the citizens of which had evacuated. A dozen Marines, secreted on the roof of a building, began calling in artillery and air strikes.

On January 30, Iraqi forces dug in despite heavy losses. Bad weather hindered air attacks, and the battle went on into the night of January 30/31. Horner diverted a three-ship cell of B-52Gs from attacking the Republican Guard and it made a difference, Lt Gen Khaled bin Sultan reporting: "A single strike by three B-52s decimated more than 80 Iraqi vehicles, lighting up the sky for miles around." Working with Marine controllers, Harriers, Hornets, and Intruders hammered columns with Maverick missiles, Rockeyes, and dumb bombs, and Marine Cobras hunted – and killed – Iraqi tanks with TOW missiles. Maj Gen Salah Aboud Mahmoud, the III Corps commander, realizing his forces now faced annihilation and denied permission to withdraw by Iraq's high command, replied bitterly, "The mother is killing her children."

Col George Muellner's Riyadh-based 4411th J-STARS Squadron (P) now proved its great worth, its two Boeing E-8As flying 10–12-hour (and sometimes longer) orbits over northeastern Saudi Arabia, their big Norden multi-function side-looking radar looking into Kuwait. The J-STARS (Joint Surveillance and Targeting Radar System) was an AWACS for the ground war, furnishing, in the words of Lt Gen Gordon "Gordy" Fornell "a real-time God's-eye view of the battle." Still experimental, only a direct request from Schwarzkopf had resulted in the two prototypes being hastily outfitted for combat and then rushed to Saudi Arabia.

AC-130H gunships and A-10As, cued by Muellner's J-STARS, wreaked havoc on Iraqi forces. A column of 71 vehicles, moving to reinforce their embattled comrades, was spotted by J-STARS and then shattered by a single AC-130 and two A-10s, that, between them, destroyed 58 vehicles: "The rest fled to the North," Muellner reported later. An Iraqi prisoner later stated that his unit suffered more losses in 30 minutes of air attack than it had in the entire eight years of the Iran–Iraq War, and a U-2R took imagery the next day showing, as Glosson recalled, "Iraqi tanks on fire across the desert, each with a plume of smoke rising."

At 0230L on January 31, Saudi National Guard and Qatari troops entered al-Khafji, retaking it by noon, freeing the 12 trapped Marines, destroying 11 T-55s and 51 BTRs, and capturing another 19 BTRs. Desultory fighting continued in the afternoon as Saudi forces and ten A-10s harried retreating Iraqi troops back across the border, having difficulty locating targets because of the obscuring smoke from burning tanks, BTRs, and other vehicles. Thus ended the Iraqi Army's incursion into Saudi Arabia. Altogether, it had lost approximately 800 tanks and APCs, over 400 artillery pieces, and several thousand troops. The US air contribution was 1,224 strike sorties: 849 USMC (69.362 percent); 174 USN (14.216 percent); and 201 USAF (16.422 percent).

The victory at al-Khafji was an important one, for it prevented Saddam from prematurely tripping the ground war. It proved to the world that Gulf Arab soldiers would courageously stand and fight without breaking against Saddam's armor; it demonstrated that what had worked in the Iran–Iraq War – frontal armored thrusts and force-on-force encounters – would not work against a Coalition that built its own campaign around air power; and it validated the joint Army-USAF E-8A J-STARS. As well, in the creative use of Pioneer RPVs for furnishing real-time intelligence and bomb-damage assessment, it signaled the "drone" as a reconnaissance system for mobile war, a role that it has subsequently fulfilled with extraordinary and at times grimly impressive results.

Finally, al-Khafji was not without Coalition loss. Maj Paul Weaver's Spirit 03, a 16th SOS AC-130H gunship, was shot down north of al-Khafji while hunting for a reported FROG-7 (Soviet 9M21) battlefield rocket battery. Ten minutes after sunrise it was hit by either an SA-7 (Sov 9K32 Strela-2) or SA-14 (Sov 9K34 Strela-3), broke up, and fell into the Gulf, killing all 14 of its crew. There was another unfortunate aspect of al-Khafji: the war's first instances of so-called "friendly fire," in which both airmen aloft and troops on the ground killed their comrades. Seven Marines perished in a light armored vehicle hit by an A-10's Maverick missile that briefly went "stupid" after launch, and then, sadly, acquired the Marine LAV. Four Marines died when a fellow LAV shot theirs with a TOW. During the liberation of al-Khafji, a USMC AH-1W destroyed an Iraqi T-55 tank and then, by mistake, a Saudi National Guard armored car. Four Saudis also perished from a Coalition bomb dropped during mixed strikes by USAF F-16s and Qatari F-1s. Finally, a Marine A-6E dropped a Rockeye munition on fellow Marines, killing one.

Victory at sea: securing the northern Persian Gulf

The victory at all-Khafji coincided with NAVCENT's victory over Saddam's small but potent navy. Given its potential for mischief, VADM Stan Arthur was determined to remove it as a threat. On January 20, he met with RADM March and CTF-154's carrier commanders, brain-storming how best to combine air and surface action to clear the Iraqi Navy out of the northern Gulf. The next day, March designated RADM Ronald J. "Zap" Zlatoper as Zulu's antisurface warfare commander. Zlatoper, commanding *Ranger's* (CV-61) battle group, prioritized sinking all Iraqi combatant vessels. He linked shared overwatch from land-based long-duration USN Lockheed P-3C Orions with AN/APS-137 inverse synthetic aperture radar (ISAR) and RAF Hawker Siddeley Nimrod MR.2P maritime patrol aircraft with Searchwater radar and GEC Sandpiper FLIRs; ship-based hunter-killer teams pairing USN SH-60B LAMPS III scouts (the hunters) with Royal Navy Westland Lynx HAS.3GM and US Army Bell OH-58D Kiowa Warrior attack helicopters (the killers); and carrier-based Lockheed S-3A/B Viking "scouts" using their AN/APS-137B radars to find vessels for

Grumman A-6E Intruders and McDonnell-Douglas F/A-18A Hornets. As well, he stepped up air strikes on naval targets including port facilities and, particularly, HY-2G Hai Ying (CSS-N-2 Silkworm) missile batteries.

On January 22, A-6Es sank a minelayer below Umm Qasr. The next day, another A-6E, Eagle Hill 503, spotted a LR-2 Suezmax-class tanker, the *Amuriyah* – nearly 160,000dwt – alongside the Mina al-Bakr oil platform, with a Saunders-Roe SR.N6c Winchester-class military hovercraft moored to its stern. The *Amuriyah* was loaded with refined petroleum, which could be released to pollute the Gulf. As well, it was believed

to be furnishing intelligence. So, when RADM March requested permission to sink it, VADM Arthur quickly assented: Eagle Hill 503 dropped cluster bombs that set it ablaze (it burned out over two weeks), while the hovercraft hastily hid under the platform. A rocket-boosted AGM-123A Skipper II LGB dropped by another A-6E flushed it out, and two other A-6Es sank it; its fortunate crew was seen rowing away.

The next day, January 24, the Iraqi Navy lost a minelayer to bombs from two A-6Es, shelling from the guided missile frigate *Curts* (FFG-38), and a *coup de grâce* strafing by an SH-60B LAMPS III helo. An Iraqi patrol boat then ran over an Iraqi-laid sea mine and blew up. On the 25th, the Coalition realized Saddam had initiated Project *Tariq*; four tankers moored at Kuwait's Mina al-Ahmadi refinery were discharging millions of gallons of crude oil into the Gulf, as was the refinery itself and the off-shore Mina al-Bakr oil platform. As it drifted with the currents, the oil slick grew to 35 miles in length and ten miles in width.

After delays from political dithering, CINCCENT anxieties, and weather, on the night of January 27, two 48th TFW (P) F-111Fs – Charger 34, crewed by pilot Capt Rick "Spanky" Walker and WSO Capt Ken Theurer, and Charger 35, crewed by pilot Maj Sammy Samson and WSO Capt Steve Williams – each scored a GBU-15V-2/32B imaging infrared (IIR) guided glide bomb hit on the manifold and pump house at al-Ahmadi, reducing the flood to a seeping trickle. To get maximum range, the F-111Fs dropped the two GBU-15s during supersonic dashes directly towards al-Ahmadi, through bursting flak from radar-cued 100mm KS-19 cannon. Fifty miles off-shore in another F-111F – Charger 32, piloted by Capt Mike Russell – WSO Capt Brad Seipel coolly controlled the GBU-15s via a joystick, cued by an AN/AXQ-14 data-link pod.

On the evening of January 26, a *Ranger* A-6E spotted two tankers transiting the Khor Abdullah passage below Umm Qasr. Arthur ordered them both sunk. But, instead of receiving the plaudits they deserved, Arthur and CTF-154's naval aviators were castigated by Gen Norman Schwarzkopf, whom Arthur recalled as "going berserk" and "yelling and screaming." It was all the more annoying because Arthur had been scrupulously following Schwarzkopf's own guidance to sink Iraq's merchant fleet, given in a December meeting. Unknown to Arthur, Schwarzkopf had then changed his mind, sending a message on January 17 forbidding attacks on anchored tankers without CINCCENT approval. But Schwarzkopf's staff had marked the message "Priority" instead of the urgent "Flash" it warranted. As a consequence – eerily recalling Gen George Marshall's Western Union telegraph warning to Pearl Harbor that arrived in the midst of the Japanese attack – the message did not get to Arthur for 11 days, by which time *Amuriyah* was a broken, flaming hulk. After this semi-comic episode, the issue blew over, but, as with Schwarzkopf's earlier Black Hole blow-up, it left scars.

If small, Iraq's Navy – 13 missile boats of four different types, including six captured from Kuwait – possessed potentially deadly striking power, armed with the Soviet P-15/20 Termit (NATO SSN-2 Styx) and the French AM-39 Exocet. It also had seven shore-based launchers and approximately 50 Chinese HY-2 (CSS-N-2 Silkworm) radar-guided missiles housed in a Kuwait City school used for storage and assembly, one of which, serial 310932, is shown after capture. (DoD)

Royal Navy Westland Lynx HAS.3GM helicopters of 815 and 829 Naval Air Squadrons, operating in detachments off British vessels, proved highly effective ship-killers employing the Bae Dynamics Sea Skua radar-homing anti-ship missile. Here is an Iraqi FPB 57 resting sedately on the bottom of the Gulf after being hit and holed by a Sea Skua-firing Lynx off HMS *Gloucester* during the so-called "Bubiyan Turkey Shoot." (DoD)

Zlatoper's strategy received its test while al-Khafji held the Coalition's attention. On January 29, at least 15 Iraqi fast patrol boats departed the Kuwaiti port of Ras al-Qulayah, heading south at high speed, likely to land commandos from the 440th Naval Infantry Brigade below al-Khafji, though possibly to retake Umm-al-Maradim, a small Kuwaiti island fort and harbor liberated that morning by a USN–USMC landing party in the name of Free Kuwait.

A patrolling VP-4 P-3C crew detected the boats, raising the alarm. Then, RAF Jaguars returning from a Silkworm strike spotted the boats, which, cheekily if unwisely, fired an IR SAM at them. In a spirited attack, the Jaguars peppered the flotilla with Canadian CRV-7 rockets and 30mm strafing, sinking one and damaging the others, two of which later sank. Then, three Royal Navy Lynx HAS.3GM helicopters from 815 Naval Air Squadron (NAS) detachments embarked on HMS *Gloucester* and *Cardiff*, and an 829 NAS "Det" off HMS *Brazen*, arrived on scene. Cued by "Dylan," a Hawker Siddeley Nimrod MR.2P, the Lynx crews fired BAe Dynamics Sea Skua radar-homing antishipping missiles, sinking two and scattering the rest. Having lost five of their flotilla and with another seven damaged, the Iraqis hastily took refuge at Khawr al Mufattah. There they remained until ignominiously sunk at dock on February 7, torn apart in a welter of 16in salvos from the battleship *Wisconsin* (BB-64), the last time that a battleship took other vessels under fire with its main battery. Even here air power played a role, a loitering VC-6 AAI RQ-2A Pioneer drone launched off *Wisconsin*'s fantail revealing its fall of shot.

Act 2 opened late that night. In a meeting in early January, Saddam had suggested the Navy should send at least some of its vessels to Iran for safe-keeping, ordering it "not [to] take part in the coming battle." On January 29, Iraq's naval leadership ordered nine vessels to Iran: four missile boats, three landing barges, an artillery boat, and a minesweeper. At 2345L, three groups of three vessels apiece departed Umm Qasr, threading their way down the Khor Abdullah passage past Bubiyan Island and into the open waters of the Gulf off the al-Faw peninsula.

Overhead were two *Ranger* A-6Es, having already attacked a suspected Silkworm site. Shortly before 0130L, the lead A-6E's bombardier-navigator, Cdr Richard Cassara, detected a "huge" radar return off al-Faw. It resolved into four vessels moving eastwards at 15–18kts. His pilot, Cdr Richard Noble, identified three as missile boats. Over 15 minutes, the two A-6Es sank three of the four. Two Canadian CF-18s, flown by Maj David Kendall and Capt Stephen Hill and on-station at 10,000ft, now took up the chase, having accepted a polite invitation from a Navy tactical coordinator who had thoughtfully queried, "Would you like to strafe a boat?" Having found the fourth, the Canadians dropped flares to illuminate it, revealing a Styx-slinging *Osa I* (Soviet Project 205) leaving a broad wake. With skill, courage, and verve, they descended perilously low, strafing it with their 20mm M61 Vulcan cannons; after their IR AIM-9 Sidewinders failed to gain a lock, one optimistically launched a radar-guided AIM-7 Sparrow, which missed by just 50ft. Shaken and holed, the *Osa I* limped off to Iranian sanctuary.

Over the next 13 hours, more vessels entered the Coalition's air–sea gauntlet, and Coalition aircraft destroyed or damaged 20 of them, including seven missile boats, three amphibious ships, a minesweeper, and nine miscellaneous others. (Briefers at an Iraqi 1993 defense conference admitted as well the curious deaths of seven generals somehow lost on the boats, unless this was to mask some Saddam score-settling infamy.) Only three vessels – the Canadian-battered *Osa I* missile boat, a *Bogomol* (Project 02065 *Vikhr*-III) gunboat, and the *Ghanda*, a *Polnocny-C* (Project 773K) tank-landing ship – reached safe harbor at Bandar Iman Khomeini. Adhering to the traditions of the sea, the US Navy rescued 20 sailors from a sunken *Polnocny-C*, the *Atika*, adding them to the growing number of prisoners held by the Coalition.

Thus ended the Battle of Bubiyan Island, the Coalition's greatest single action against the Iraqi Navy. But as with al-Khafji, its victory came at a price. On February 2, Heartless 531, a VA-36 A-6E, reported taking fire from the north shore of Kuwait Bay, including an inbound IR-missile. A search discovered wreckage and a fuel slick off Faylakah Island, and the searchers came under fire, RAF Jaguars promptly and terminally silencing the offending AAA sites.

Phase III: "preparing the battlefield" or "destroying the battlefield?"

The date for G-Day – liberating Kuwait – depended on how badly the Phase III air campaign had weakened Saddam's forces: what armies called "preparing the battlefield." "When the bombing started," the GWAPS effectiveness report found, "transportation began to crumble. [Troops] ran short of water, food, fuel, and all spare parts. Some units had their supply stocks destroyed. Training in the units ceased." By Day 21, February 6, LGBs had dropped 22 of 24 critical highway bridges. Eventually, by war's end, LGBs had dropped 41 of 54 key bridges, and 31 pontoon bridge "work-arounds." More significantly, the regime's ability to move supplies to Kuwait was cut by over 90 percent, from 216,000 metric tons per day to just 20,000 metric tons per day. Anti-vehicle attacks created further problems. One mechanized brigade lost 60 percent of all its vehicles including three-quarters of its water and fuel tankers. Another division lost 70 out of 80 trucks. As reported by Iraqi sources, by late January supplies stockpiled at corps and division level "could not be regularly distributed below those levels," and units began herding camels to replace trucks. A log entry for February 10 reported that at Abu Talib (Tallil AB) "there is only enough food for the officers," a sad if

Bridge attacks, such as this railroad bridge dropped by air attack, severely disrupted Iraqi mobility and resupply, something repeating the experience of previous wars. But while bridges in those wars had required hundreds and perhaps thousands of sorties before they were finally dropped, bridge attacks in the new era of precision air attack typically meant a single mission by an aircraft carrying two laser-guided bombs. (DoD)

telling commentary on how Iraqi Air Force officers both regarded and treated their enlisted personnel.

From the Iraqi perspective, B-52Gs and A-10As were the most feared Gulf attackers, "Buffs," because of the profound terror, shock, and fury induced by a three-ship cell distributing over 57 tons of bombs across a target, and A-10As, because of their ubiquitous whining presence. Brig Gen Talal Shafiq Mohamed, chief of staff of the 30th Infantry Division, stated air attacks convinced senior officers "resistance was futile as they were 'against the world.'"

SAC's B-52Gs flew 1,741 sorties and dropped 72,000 bombs totaling 27,000 tons (most were aging M-117 750lb general-purpose bombs, a total of 43,435 being dropped), without sustaining a combat loss (though some were peppered by Iraqi defenses over the first three nights until they went to high altitude). Every three hours, all day and night, over the entire war, a cell of B-52Gs would bomb an Iraqi division. One such strike on the Republican Guard's 7th Adnan Motorized Infantry Division triggered such a massive secondary explosion that a US Space Command DSP satellite detected the flash from its stationary orbit.

Leaflet drops boosted the psychological impact of B-52G bombings, two Iraqi division commanders, Brig Gen Ibrahim Adwan Abdul Hussein of the 27th Infantry Division, and Brig Gen Ahmed Hamid Suleiman of the 31st Infantry Division, considering them second only to the bombings in triggering desertions, particularly since they promised water, food, and safety. Leaflets warned units they would be bombed the next day; a B-52G cell would then do so; the day after another unit would receive a leaflet drop warning them they would be hit, and referencing the previous bombing. The result built fear, uncertainty, and stress, the enticement being a suggestion soldiers walk south towards Coalition forces, or west towards Mecca.

One veteran of the Iran–Iraq War singled out B-52G bombing as "the worst thing he had ever experienced." Iraqi Brig Gen Saheb Mohammed Alaw, commander of the 48th Infantry Division, blamed B-52Gs for most desertions (an estimated 160,000 troops). Another Iraqi credited B-52G attacks for his surrender: "But your position was never attacked by B-52s," his interrogator replied. "That is true," he stated, "but I saw one that had been attacked."

At war's end, Coalition soldiers escorting POWs repeatedly commented on how the sight or sound of an airplane would trigger a flinch, a sudden crouch, or a panicked look skyward. Studying the air campaign's psychological impact, then-Gp Capt Andrew P.N. Lambert found the constant threat of air attack induced feelings of fear, isolation, persecution, depression, abandonment, suicide, and betrayal: half of all POWs had contemplated murdering their officers. To others, unnerved by seemingly endless bombing (irrespective of any damage) and the jarring sound and worrying sight of airplanes, the certainty of death became preferable to living uncertainly in fear of it, and so, tragically, they took their own lives.

For the US Army, its pre-G-Day aircraft of choice was the A-10A, designed specifically as a low-altitude Warsaw Pact tank-killer. In over nearly 8,100 sorties, A-10A pilots claimed approximately 1,000 tanks, 2,000 other vehicles, and 1,200 artillery pieces. For artillery strikes, A-10As typically dropped air burst-fuzed Mk-82s out of a 45–60-degree dive (Mk-20 Rockeye CBUs proved much less useful, many producing a high "dud" rate). The AGM-65B/D Maverick was the weapon of first resort against tanks and APCs, because it afforded greater accuracy from a safe distance than the much-touted GAU-8 30mm cannon. Altogether, A-10As fired 4,801 Mavericks, 90 percent of all Mavericks fired by the USAF in the war. Out of a 30-degree dive, pilots could fire the electro-optical AGM-65B at a slant range up to 3.7 miles (6km), or an even further 5.75 miles (9km) if firing the imaging infrared (IIR) AGM-65D. Firing the 30mm GAU-8 with accuracy meant closing to a slant-range of just 4,000ft, putting the A-10A deep in the midst of the Iraq Army's plethora of low-altitude defenses.

Despite its heavily armored design, Iraqi air defenders shot down five (and shot up a sixth so badly it could not be repaired), damaging 14 others. Attacking Republican Guard divisions

The mobile Soviet ZSU-23/4 quad-barrel 23mm light antiaircraft cannon combined a RPK-2 (NATO Gun Dish) fire control radar with an electromechanical calculator. It had an altitude capability of 6,000ft (1,830m) and could fire up to 4,000rpm (rounds per minute, i.e. 1,000 rounds per barrel per minute), though its practical sustained firing rate was 800rpm (200 per barrel per minute). First encountered by the West in the 1973 Arab–Israeli War, it proved a devastatingly effective low-altitude air defense system. Iraq had approximately 20 different kinds of antiaircraft cannon and heavy machine guns, the Shilka arguably being the most dangerous of them all. (DoD)

was particularly risky. On Day 30, February 15, CENTAF lost two with a third, flown by Col David Sawyer, commander of the 354th TFW (P), badly damaged. Thinking "Loneliness is climbing at 200kts with the nearest friendlies 55 miles away," he passed over F-16Cs attacking just inside Kuwait and suddenly, like Saul on the road to Damascus, was struck with a blinding insight: "A-10s over the Republican Guards and F-16s in the southern KTO doesn't compute." Horner, increasingly leery of A-10A survivability, concurred, immediately restricting it to within 20nm (23 statute miles, 37km) of the Kuwaiti–Saudi border. Only after G-Day, when retreating Iraqis abandoned their dense AAA and SAM defenses, would the A-10A (quoting the 354th TFW (P)'s wartime chronology) "roam the battlefield with near-total impunity."

As February opened, then, Horner and Glosson recognized Phase III's antitank, artillery, and APC effort faced three major challenges: the inaccuracy inherent in dropping bombs from medium altitudes; the vulnerability of AC-130H gunships to SAMs; and the disturbing vulnerability of USAF A-10As and USMC AV-8Bs in the very role for which both had been designed, namely low-altitude battlefield air support against defended armored and mechanized forces. The solution was to capitalize on a triumvirate of LGB-dropping precision attackers: the USAF's General Dynamics F-111F Aardvarks with Pave Tack and McDonnell-Douglas F-15E Strike Eagle with LANTIRN, and the USN–USMC's TRAM/MSIP Grumman A-6E Intruders.

On cold January nights, F-111F crews noticed their Pave Tack FLIR clearly showed heat signatures from vehicles and artillery. Lt Col Joe Bob Phillips, a planner in the Black Hole, realized combining Pave Tack imaging plus 500lb GBU-12 LGBs – largely unused because of their relatively small explosive power, and thus available by the thousands – could make the F-111F a devastating tank and artillery killer, operating well above most Iraqi defenses. Glosson concurred, ordering Col Tom Lennon's 48th TFW (P) to test the idea. On the night of February 5, Lennon led two F-111Fs, Charger 07 and 08, in an attack upon the RG's al-Medina armored division. Seven of their eight bombs scored direct hits. Horner, reviewing the FLIR tapes, wrote, "[they] ought to be required viewing at the Army War College and A-10 Fighter Weapons School – [a] classic of how to do the job right." He immediately redirected the F-111Fs to "tank-plinking." "I told the troops 'General Schwarzkopf does

An Iraqi T-55 tank destroyed by air attack. "Tank plinking" by F-111Fs, F-15Es, A-6Es, and A-10s, whether by laser-guided bombs or by precision Maverick missiles, shocked Iraqi tankers with the effectiveness of air-delivered guided munitions. "In the war with Iran my tank was my friend and I could sleep in it at night," one complained, "but in this war they just kept blowing up." Prudent crews bedded down well distant from their vehicles. (DoD)

not want you to call it tank-plinking,'" Horner said, "and that way I ensured that it will forever be known as tank-plinking."

By the war's fourth week, more than half of all the 48th's sorties went towards tank-plinking. Operating in concert with Muellner's E-8A J-STARs, Lennon's F-111Fs thereafter dropped more than 2,500 500lb GBU-12s. One night, 20 F-111Fs dropping 80 GBU-12s destroyed 77 armored and other mechanized vehicles of Iraq's 52nd Armored Division. On February 9, the 48th's maintainers put up 40 F-111Fs that then destroyed over 100 armored vehicles. (By that time, Iraqi tankers were sleeping well away from their tanks.) On February 22, the 48th attacked the artillery-heavy 47th Infantry Division, destroying over 100 artillery pieces.

The 48th TFW (P) flew its strangest F-111F plinking mission just before G-Day. In the 1980s, Iraq purchased 24 Blue Bird Wanderlodge luxury motor coaches. Saddam Hussein had used them for senior staff transportation, and was filmed inside one shortly after the opening of the war. Intelligence spotted one outside al-Qa'im in western Iraq – and near a command bunker. On February 22, four F-111Fs, two with GBU-12s to plink the coach and two with hardened 2,000lb LGBs to destroy the bunker, flew off in the predawn for al-Qa'im. All four "shacked" their targets. Strikes like this fed Saddam's paranoia that enemies were out to kill him. He grew morose and unpredictable, his inner circle increasingly aware that what happened to Iraq, its military – excepting the Republican Guard, essential to his personal and political survival – and its people, concerned Saddam far less (if at all) than staying alive and in charge.

CENTAF credited the 48th TFW (P)'s F-111F pilots and WSOs with 1,500 vehicle or equipment kills, including 920 tanks and 252 artillery pieces. At the height of tank-plinking, they were scoring upwards of 150 armor kills nightly, a rate per sortie seven times greater than the A-10A. Closing fast were Col Hal Hornburg's 4th TFW (P) F-15E crews; on several occasions, pairs of Strike Eagles, each armed with eight GBU-12s, destroyed 16 vehicles. Over southeastern Iraq and Kuwait, Navy and Marine A-6Es scored well on their own anti-artillery and anti-vehicle strikes. For both the Marines and the Navy, the A-6E – fighting its last war, like the smaller A-7 – was a dependably heavy puncher, attacking fielded forces, airfields, missile sites, and the Iraqi Navy, and its crews deserve greater recognition than they have received.

Precision air attack profoundly affected Iraqi troops exposed to it. It convinced them their tanks were no refuge, breaking the bond of warrior and weapon. As the Coalition edged closer to G-Day and the toll of Iraqi armor, artillery, and other vehicles destroyed by precision air attack rose ever higher, Lt Col David Deptula put up a sign inside the Black Hole: "We are not 'Preparing the Battlefield,'" it read, "We are '*Destroying* the Battlefield.'"

The intelligence debate

The intelligence community disagreed. On January 31 ARCENT's Lt Gen John Yeosock briefed Schwarzkopf that overall Iraq military power stood at 93 percent, and that Saddam's Republican Guard was even stronger, retaining 99 percent of its armored vehicles, 98 percent of its tanks, and 99 percent of its artillery. Examining satellite imaging, the Central Intelligence Agency generally concurred, concluding Saddam's armored forces retained

92 percent combat power. In contrast, using all-source intelligence, CENTCOM believed the Iraqi army had started with 4,280 tanks in theater, and since then, Coalition airmen had destroyed 1,400, about a third. ARCENT's and the CIA's percentages defied common sense, running counter to what was readily visible on nightly FLIR images from F-111Fs, F-15Es, and A-6Es.

The disparity fueled Schwarzkopf's suspicion that Washington's intelligence "experts" were doing more harm than good. "From the first day of *Desert Storm*," he recalled, "they had us going in circles." So exacting were analysts' standards that he complained "Vehicles must be on their back like a dead cockroach" before they would assess them as destroyed; worse, he told the US Senate after the war, "by the time you got done reading many of the intelligence estimates you received, no matter what happened, they would have been right. And that's not helpful."

In truth, though, assessing tanks did pose a challenge. A 30mm depleted uranium round or a Maverick missile typically made a small entry hole, burning the tank out. But unless strike video captured the hit, or the tank's own exploding ammunition blew the turret off, a recce photograph taken afterwards showed a seemingly undamaged tank. In one case, analysts denied a claim until a keen-eyed interpreter noticed the entire turret had been shifted sideways by a foot.

There was more: on February 3, Lt Col Rick Lewis discovered both ARCENT and MARCENT intelligence analysts only counted A-10A claims, dismissing those by aircrew of other aircraft, including LGB-dropping F-111Fs, F-15Es, and A-6Es. Glosson and Horner protested vociferously, and Schwarzkopf ordered analysts to accept all claims buttressed by strike video. In the fashion of Washington policy disputes, self-serving anonymous sources leaked the numbers controversy to friendly media. Retired generals, journalists, and think-tank cognoscenti immediately started trading opinions and numbers with the burning-eyed fervor of medieval Scholastics arguing the sum of angels on heads of pins.

The debate threatened to delay the ground campaign for weeks. If ARCENT was correct, it would take until D + 100 – April 26, 1991 – before Schwarzkopf could commence G-Day. Frustrated, Glosson directed his planners to look elsewhere for reliable and rapid intelligence

A 1704th Strategic Reconnaissance Squadron (Provisional) Lockheed TR-1A (SN 80-1084) departs Taif on a reconnaissance mission. The TR-1A, structurally identical to the U-2R, furnished stand-off tactical intelligence, employing the side-looking near-real-time high-resolution Advanced Synthetic Aperture Radar System-II (ASARS-II). Shooting down a TR-1A or an E-3 AWACS was a goal of the Iraqi fighter force. (DoD)

support. They turned to Col John Warden's Checkmate and the Joint Staff J-2, RADM John M. "Mike" McConnell. Together, Warden and McConnell got timely intelligence to the Black Hole, Glosson writing of McConnell that "He will never know how important he has been and will be to our overall success." On the eve of G-Day, CENTCOM confidently estimated that Iraq had lost 1,800 tanks, 950 APCs, and 1,500 artillery pieces. Enemy forces immediately before VII Corps were at approximately 45 percent of their pre-war combat strength, while those in front of the 1st Marine Expeditionary Force were about 70 percent, reflecting the smaller number of LGBs and missiles used in attacking them. Most importantly, the intelligence debate did not delay liberating Kuwait, and G-Day was D + 38, not D + 100.

The al-Firdos bunker bombing

On February 8–9, Dick Cheney, Colin Powell, and Paul Wolfowitz visited CENTCOM, meeting with Schwarzkopf, Waller, and the commanders of CENTAF, ARCENT, MARCENT, and NAVCENT. Afterwards, Cheney, Powell, and Schwarzkopf set the date for G-Day. Using an input from Horner, Schwarzkopf suggested February 21, with a three-day window. Cheney and Powell agreed, and afterwards so did President Bush. By mid-February, Saddam Hussein was attempting to reconstitute effective command and control of his military and the organs of state control, and the decision put greater urgency on striking leadership targets ("L targets"). On the night of February 12/13, F-117As returned to Baghdad, bombing 15 of them.

One was Target L30: the al-Firdos command, control, and communications bunker. Two F-117As bombed it with a single GBU-27 apiece. What intelligence analysts – and planners, dependent on them – did not know was that it doubled as a bomb shelter for families of the governing elite. They would have been safer anywhere but there: the Coalition never considered urban area bombing (the reason to seek shelter), and using a legitimate target as a shelter made tragedy inevitable. The bombs killed most inhabitants, the Iraqi regime reporting the death toll as 204.

CNN broke the story, and United Nations' Secretary-General Javier Pérez de Cuéller unhelpfully accused the Coalition of committing "war crimes." Characteristically concerned

A McDonnell-Douglas F/A-18C Hornet of *Saratoga*'s VFA-81 approaching an Air Force KC-135 tanker during a *Desert Shield* exercise. This aircraft is the F/A-18C that, as Modex 403, was lost with pilot Cdr Scott Speicher on opening night; VFA-81 got its own back and more the next day when squadron mates Mark Fox and Mongo Mongillo shot down two Fishbeds while enroute to bomb al-Wallid airbase (H-3). (DoD)

with image and politics, Colin Powell informed Schwarzkopf "there was intensive media interest in our overnight bombing of a command-and-control bunker in Baghdad." In turn, Schwarzkopf confided to Glosson that "The Chairman is going ballistic," adding, "He's going to minimize Baghdad bombing from here on." Baghdad and its environs were placed off-limits for ten days, not back on the ATO until the end of the war. "Al-Firdos," Glosson subsequently wrote, "was the nail in the coffin for the strategic campaign."

Phase IV: to G-Day and afterwards

As February progressed, airmen focused on attacking forces and battlefield infrastructure in advance of G-Day. Precision strikes by A-6Es, F-15Es, and F-111Fs targeted artillery and armor, and cells of B-52Gs continued bombing the Republican Guard (and started bombing breaching areas). F-117As bombed pumping stations to deny fuel for fire trenches and traps (which AV-8Bs ignited with Mk-77 napalm canisters). F-117As and F-111Fs targeted communications to deny Iraqi commanders use of land-lines, forcing them to use radio, which SIGINT could exploit.

The Coalition also ran complex deception operations to convince Iraqi generals that naval forces would execute an amphibious landing, including having USAF MC-130Es drop three massive 15,000lb BLU-82 bombs on Faylakah Island, and the battleships *Missouri* (BB-63) and *Wisconsin* (BB-64) bombard Iraqi shore positions. In a case of cosmic irony, at 0435L on February 18, the flagship of the Persian Gulf mine-sweeping flotilla, the amphibious assault ship *Tripoli* (LPH-10) itself ran over a contact mine that severely damaged it. Then, at 0715L, the guided missile cruiser *Princeton* (CG-59) struck another, suffering even greater damage. Had sea-states been higher, each might have been lost. Fortunately, no sailors perished (though seven were injured), and both *Tripoli* and *Princeton* limped into Bahrain for repairs. On a happier note, on the 20th, the *Valley Forge* (CG-52) vectored a VS-32 Lockheed S-3B Viking (aka "Hoover," from its whine) onto a gunboat, which the plane's crew promptly sank with three Mk-82 500lb bombs; another Viking crew, from VS-24, bombed an air defense site out of existence.

Captured documents reveal that in the last week in January, Iraq's military intelligence service, the GMID, had detected the shift of Coalition forces westward beyond Hafar

A mixed column of vehicles caught and destroyed fleeing Kuwait. Concentrated air attacks triggered by Boeing E-8A J-STARS imagery of the Iraqi III Corps panicked retreat towards the Kuwaiti frontier and led to many scenes such as this. (DoD)

al-Batin, but its puzzled analysts could not comprehend why. On the eve of G-Day, GMID still had no idea where and when the Coalition's blow would fall. They learned on Day 39, Sunday, February 24. That day, across an approximately 350-mile front running from the Persian Gulf deep into the Arabian heartland, Coalition forces invaded Iraq. In the west was the US Army's XVIII Airborne Corps under Lt Gen Gary E. Luck with Brig Gen Bernard Janvier's 6th (FR) Light Armored Division. In the middle was Lt Gen Frederick M. "Freddy" Franks Jr's VII Corps, including Maj Gen Rupert Smith's 1st (BR) Armored Division. In the east below Kuwait was Lt Gen Khaled bin Sultan's Joint Force Command-East (JFC-E) and Joint Force Command-North (JFC-N). Sandwiched between them was Lt Gen Walter Boomer's 1st Marine Expeditionary Force (I MEF), including the US Army's 1st (Tiger) Brigade.

The weather was miserable: fog, cloud, rain, and wind, made worse in the southeast by the pervasive stench, grimy residue, and oily smoke of 650 flaming wells, pools, and well-heads torched by Iraqi soldiers. The gouting plumes – all foul and some lethally poisonous – turned day to night, forming a single great shameful cloud that streamed across the Gulf into Iran.

Ignoring the weather, Horner and Glosson ordered their airmen aloft. "There are people's lives depending on our ability to help them if help is required," Horner wrote. "Up over the battlefield, it's time to go to work." Glosson ordered "Close Air Support and Air Interdiction missions are not [to be] weather canceled by some decision-maker removed from the scene." Thus, despite the weather, on Phase IV's first day, Coalition airmen flew 3,280 sorties, the war's highest daily total, including 1,200 targeting armored vehicles.

In the west, at 0100L, French scouts crossed the frontier, followed at 0400L by Brig Gen Bernard Janvier's 6th Light Armored Division. Aérospatiale SA 341F2 Gazelle helicopters scouted ahead, destroying Iraqi tanks, vehicles, bunkers, and outposts with Euromissile HOT missiles. Janvier established Forward Operating Base Rochambeau, then pressed on to seize as-Salman ("Objective White") before halting, having secured the left flank. Simultaneously, 300 CH-47 Chinooks and UH-60 Blackhawks of the Army's 18th Aviation Brigade, screened by OH-58 C/D Kiowa Scouts, AH-64A Apache, and AH-1F/S Cobra gunships, lifted the 101st Airborne Division (Air Assault) to seize a section of Iraq, Forward Operating Base Cobra. The US Army's 24th Mechanized Infantry Division under Maj Gen Barry McCaffrey then crossed the frontier at 1500L, quickly pushed past FOB Cobra, and continued deep into Iraq, beginning a record run that would take it on a curving course ending just west of Basra.

In the center, the first elements of Franks' VII Corps crossed into Iraq on the 24th, with Smith's 1st (BR) Armored Division following at 0200L on February 25, but thereafter Franks

The McDonnell-Douglas (formerly Hughes) AH-64A Apache gunship was one of the Coalition's real strengths against Iraqi tanks and mechanized forces. Flying a little more than a soldier's height, armed with Hellfire laser-guided missiles, pods of Hydra-70 flechette rockets, and a 30mm rapid firing "chain gun," the ungainly looking Apache would prove itself a lethal master of the battlefield. (DoD)

moved slowly, to Schwarzkopf's displeasure. In contrast, Lt Gen Walt Boomer's I MEF entered Kuwait on schedule at 0400L on the 24th and, despite berms and mine-fields, its two divisions made rapid progress: by day's end, I MEF was just 15 miles short of Kuwait City. Weather and oil smoke disrupted a planned Marine helicopter insertion of Task Force X-Ray, a light anti-tank force, behind Iraqi lines. After waiting for hours at "Lonesome Dove" (a Marine forward air base near Al Khanjar, Saudi Arabia), 52 CH-46 Sea Knight and CH-53 Sea Stallion helicopters lifted TF X-Ray's 40 light anti-armor vehicles and 130 Marines, escorted by AH-1J and AH-1W gunships. At the start, gusts rolled-over a CH-46, fortunately without injuries. The glare of oil fires hindered situational awareness, and night vision goggles didn't help. In the murk helicopters narrowly missed each other, and finally, wisely, the mission was canceled. Low on fuel, many CH-46s landed in the desert, and one CH-53 that did make base touched down so hard its nose gear punched through the cockpit floor.

Coalition troops advanced behind massive artillery barrages, screaming rocket artillery, low-flying attack aircraft, and their armies' own troop lift and helicopter gunships. Greeting them were dozens, then hundreds, and soon thousands of Iraqi soldiers, many advancing holding one of the millions of leaflets dropped by Coalition aircraft promising safe treatment. The prisoners were almost uniformly malnourished, sick, thirsty, infested with lice, and covered in sores. Six weeks of bombing had left them cowering and fearful, looking skyward with anxiety every time a plane or helicopter passed overhead. "They were scared stiff of the planes," British Army Cpl Rex Butt recalled. "Every time a plane came over they were terrified."

Saddam's inner circle took the first reports of attacks with surprising complacency, but by day's end, he recognized the danger, remarking, "If it were not for their air forces, our Republican Guard units would have come out and slaughtered them." In response, the Iraqi Navy sent an Exocet-armed Aérospatiale SA 321H Super Frelon to sink any Coalition ship, but (according to attendees at a 1993 Iraq naval conference), the Frelon "was exposed to an accident" before it could do so. In reality, US naval intelligence had learned of the plan (likely through SIGINT intercepts), and pre-empted the attack. Lt Cdr Jeffrey S. "Bones" Ashby, VFA-195's ace AGM-62 Walleye I/II glide-bomb dropper – he had trashed Iraqi naval headquarters at Umm Qasr with one – launched off *Midway*, and, having found the SA 321H, dropped and steered a Walleye so precisely that it hit between the Frelon's engines, blowing it to pieces.

Iraq eventually did take a missile shot at the fleet, at 0452L on February 27, in the midst of a bombardment by the battleship *Missouri* (BB-63). A site near al-Fintas, Kuwait, launched two HY-2G Hai Ying (NATO CSS-2 Silkworm) missiles. One immediately crashed in the sea, but the second, trailing a mesmerizingly flaming exhaust, continued onwards, towards the battleship. The *Missouri* fired rapidly blooming chaff, flares, and decoys, as did the frigate *Jarrett* (FFG-33), which fired on the missile with its Phalanx close-in weapon system (CIWS). Fired in auto-engagement mode, the Phalanx targeted *Missouri*'s chaff plume, not the missile, and, adding insult to injury, hit the battleship's upper works with four of its decelerating 20mm tungsten rounds, fortunately without inflicting injury or death. Thanks to a fast-working operations team and adroit maneuvering by Cdr Philip Wilcocks RN, the Type 42 destroyer HMS *Gloucester* (D96, assigned to *Missouri* as her dedicated anti-air escort) fired two rocket-boosted ramjet-powered BAe Sea Dart Mod 2 SAMs, downing the HY-2G in an explosion so huge that observers feared *Gloucester* had been hit and blown up. *Missouri*, seeking pay-back, launched an AAI RQ-2A that located the battery. Thus informed, the "Mighty Mo" fired 30 16in rounds that obliterated it together with its bold if ill-fated launch crew.

The ground successes of the first day continued over the next three, to the end of the war, though Franks – a Montgomery, not a Patton – persisted on moving far more slowly than either Schwarzkopf or his own tankers desired. On the night of February 25, J-STARS detected hundreds of vehicles leaving Kuwait City and moving towards Basra and Safwan: the Iraqi III Corps was "bugging out" to avoid Walt Boomer's rapidly advancing I MEF and Khaled bin Sultan's JFC-East. Glosson immediately ordered Strike Eagle attacks. As the Air Force's official history of the Kuwaiti campaign notes:

> Beginning at about midnight, two ship cells of F-15Es began attacking the convoys every 15 minutes. After 0300L, the 4th TFW began turning Strike Eagles from Al Kharj with combined-effects munitions (CEMs) while armorers began preparing F-16Cs at Al Minhad with CBUs, readying them for operations after daylight. At 0400L the TACC directed three B-52s against a marshaling area just north of the Euphrates. At the same hour, 12 more F-15Es also joined the attack, keeping pressure on the Iraqis in northwestern Kuwait and southern Iraq until 0700L, when the F-16 Killer Scouts would arrive for their daytime work. Even though most of the Strike Eagle crews already had flown five- or six-hour missions that night, they stepped up to the job. One officer recalled, "Every jet that could fly, every guy that could walk to an airplane, basically, went on that mission, out of crew rest."

"We found the lead guys on both roads that ran north out of Kuwait City and northeast," one F-15E pilot said, adding, "And it was a 30-mile traffic jam on both roads. And then the E models went in and, basically, destroyed everything on both roads for 30 miles." Three AC-130A gunships, Ghost 6, Ghost 7, and Ghost 10, also joined in with their own devastating fire power.

On the 26th, the 1st Marine Division arrived at Kuwait International Airport, while the 2nd Marine Division and the Army's Tiger Brigade pressed north, to Mutla Ridge, destroying numerous tanks. Before them lay (in an Army summary) "hundreds of shattered enemy vehicles of all types." One Army officer remarked afterwards, "The Air Force just blew the shit out of both roads," though many strikes were executed by CVW-2's naval aviators, one calling them "the mother of all target opportunities." Mercifully, though there were an estimated 1,400 destroyed, damaged, and abandoned armored vehicles and military trucks (and hundreds more of civilian trucks, vans, and automobiles), actual human casualties were low, in the order of several hundred instead of many thousands. With a large number having already been exposed to air attack, prudent drivers and passengers had wasted no time abandoning their treasure and taking to the desert, leaving vehicles to go up in flames. Nevertheless, media quickly dubbed it the "Highway of Death," and the images that were brought to mind were sufficient to cause President George H.W. Bush and Chairman of the JCS, Gen Colin Powell, to end the war as quickly as possible.

That day, Franks' VII Corps finally confronted the Republican Guard, in the first of a series of sharp, highly lethal actions – 73 Easting, Medina Ridge, Objective Norfolk, the Causeway – during which the Abrams and Challenger demonstrated their overwhelming superiority over the T-72 and any earlier vintage tank. In all these, both sides fought with courage and tenacity but, again, technology and training won the day.

If the previous 39-day air campaign had showcased fixed-wing aviation, the advance into Iraq showcased the deadliness of the helicopter with antitank missiles. British Army Lynxes blasted tanks and mechanized vehicles with TOW missiles, and French Army Gazelles (sometimes in formations up to 25 machines) firing HOT missiles scored 127 hits against Iraqi vehicles and equipment for an expenditure of 180 missiles. In the so-called "Battle of the Causeway" on February 27, Apache crews from the 4th Battalion of the 229th Aviation Brigade destroyed approximately 50 tanks in a single engagement, scoring 102 hits for an expenditure of 107 Hellfire missiles. The teaming of Kiowas and Apaches, and sometimes Kiowas with older AH-1S Cobras, claimed as many as 20 Iraqi tanks and vehicles per mission, and the Marines enjoyed equivalent successes with their TOW-armed AH-1Ws and older AH-1Js.

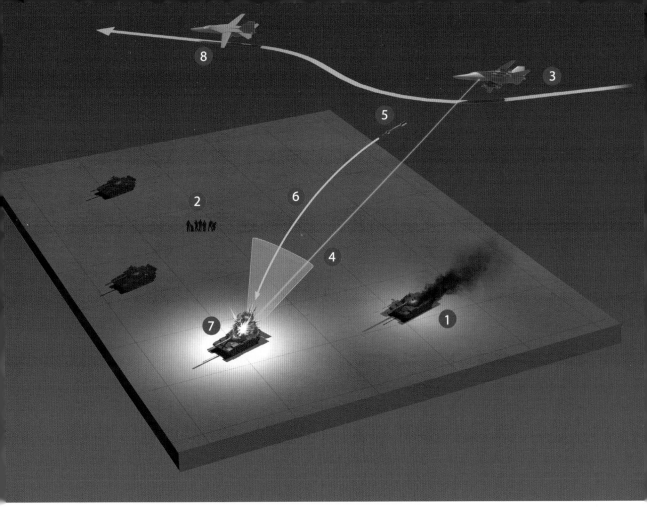

ABOVE LASER-GUIDED BOMB DELIVERY

Of all precision munitions, laser-guided bombs (LGBs) were the most effective. The F-111F proved particularly deadly. What became known as "tank plinking" began on the night of February 5 when two F-111Fs from the 48th TFW (P) attacked the Republican Guard's al-Medina armored division.

1 An Iraqi tank burns in its berm, having previously been hit by an F-111F's GBU-12.

2 Conditioned by previous attacks, Iraqi tank crews encamp away from their tanks.

3 An F-111F armed with four GBU-12 Paveway II LGBs flies over Iraqi fielded forces at an altitude of 20,200ft to avoid Iraqi small arms and light antiaircraft fire. Having radar-navigated to the target area ("kill box") and updated the F-111F's inertial navigation system (INS), the Weapon Systems Operator (WSO) scans the battlespace with a 132x176 milliradian Infrared (IR) display. Having located a deployed Iraqi T-55 tank in a protective berm because of its warm thermal signature in contrast to surrounding terrain, he fires the Pave Tack's targeting laser at the tank.

4 The laser light scattered off the tank creates a target energy "basket" that the laser seeker of the GBU 12 can detect.

5 With the laser locked on the targeted tank, the F-111F crew releases a single GBU-12, dropped at an altitude of 17,800ft. As the bomb drops away, broad tail fins spring open from the tail, enhancing its aerodynamic performance.

6 The F-111F WSO continues lasing the target as the GBU-12 falls to earth, its seeker homing on the laser spot on the tank.

7 Approximately 15 seconds after release, the bomb impacts and destroys the tank. Paveway II GBU 12 LGBs dropped from 15,000ft demonstrated an 88 percent hit rate during the Gulf War, with an average circular error probable (CEP) of 3.6ft (1.1m) off the aimpoint (i.e. the laser spot).

8 Having destroyed one tank, and with three GBU-12s remaining, the F-111F crew resumes searching for another target.

Endgame

Coalition casualties had been low, save for air and land friendly fire. USAF A-10As mistakenly destroyed two British Warrior infantry fighting vehicles, killing nine, and numerous cases of ground-to-ground friendly fire occurred between ground forces, particularly the US Army. All through the 27th, the Coalition consolidated its expanding victory over Saddam's now-shattered forces in Kuwait. That day, Colin Powell called Schwarzkopf and came right to the point: "We ought to be talking about a cease fire." Then, referencing the "Highway of Death," he added, "The reports make it look like wanton killing." They decided to continue the war for an additional day to give air power the chance to savage the Republican Guard forces north of Kuwait that were moving back into Iraq. But Powell then called back and informed Schwarzkopf that President Bush wanted to make an announcement at 2100 Washington time on February 27 (0500L in Riyadh on February 28) announcing a cease fire at 0800L in Riyadh on February 28. Schwarzkopf agreed, and so combat operations came to a halt. Concerned that the Iraqi military get the message that they were still under watch, Schwarzkopf told Horner to maintain an air presence over Baghdad. "We have two options," Horner replied, "subsonic or supersonic." Schwarzkopf chose supersonic and thereafter, the characteristic double-crack "Boom-BOOM" of sonic shocks echoed through the streets and alleys of Baghdad both day and night.

At a meeting at Safwan on March 3, Schwarzkopf and Khaled bin Sultan met with Iraqi Lt Gen Hashim Ahmad al-Jabburi, the Army vice chief of staff, and Maj Gen Salah Aboud Mahmoud, the III Corps commander. Coldly and formally, Schwarzkopf dictated the Coalition's terms, brooking no discussion. Both Iraqis were dismayed at how many of their soldiers were in Coalition custody – eventually totaling 87,000 – and how far Coalition forces had advanced , leaving the meeting (in the words of an official DoD report) "noticeably more subdued" than when they arrived.

For many, the announcement of a ceasefire brought mixed feelings. While Saddam's forces in Kuwait had been shattered – 39 of 42 Iraqi divisions were combat ineffective or destroyed – and Kuwait City had been liberated by Lt Gen Khaled bin Sultan's JFC, the Republican Guard possessed powerful formations that remained untouched largely because Powell and Bush had convinced themselves the war must be concluded lest people consider it "wanton killing;" VII Corps had moved so slowly that its commendably aggressive tankers could not close and destroy the Guard sooner than they did; and finally, on February 27, VII Corps placed the Fire Support Coordination Line (FSCL) so far forward – all the way to the Euphrates river – that it became a shield protecting the Medina and Hammurabi divisions as they made their way home. Coalition land forces were not in position to attack them, and Coalition airmen, because of the FSCL, couldn't. The combination of these saved two Republican Guard divisions that would, in coming months, strengthen Saddam Hussein's hold over Iraq.

As for Saddam, as reported by Gen Wafiq al-Samarri, Iraq's former chief of military intelligence, as the Coalition's armored forces advanced across Iraq, he grew more and more despondent. But then, learning that Bush had ordered a ceasefire, he proclaimed, "We have won!" To his mind, winning was staying in power, and by that measure so he had.

Ironically, by the Coalition's measure – removing Iraq from Kuwait and destroying its ability to invade and intimidate its neighbors – the Coalition had won. So both sides, at the end of a 43-day high-tempo high-technology war, claimed victory, though for very different reasons.

AFTERMATH AND ANALYSIS

On May 29, 1991, President Bush spoke to the graduating class of the Air Force Academy at Colorado Springs. "Gulf Lesson One," he said, "is the value of air power." Indeed, air played the predominant role in shattering the Iraqi military. A postwar study by the RAND Corporation noted: "In the past, air has been a support element that contributed around 10 to 20 percent to the outcome of the land battle. In this conflict, Coalition air forces were responsible for 50 percent or more of the enemy ground force's losses. This represents a significant shift in the contribution of the respective forces on the outcome of the air-land battle."

Desert Storm constituted both the pinnacle of Cold War air power, and the departure point that led to a new era in power projection. In a larger sense, the war discredited all who had pronounced over four decades that ending the Cold War would immediately launch a golden age of world peace. At the end of 1989, pundits argued about how to spend the "peace dividend" from ending Cold War military spending, some suggesting it was time to fold up the US Air Force and the Royal Air Force. By the end of 1990, they were arguing about how many casualties the Saddam regime might inflict on the international forces arrayed against it, and, for the most part, dismissing any expectation that Coalition air power might make a significant difference.

Ironically, within weeks of the end of the war, when it was evident to the average citizen how differently the war had gone compared to pre-war predictions, many pundits were now already spinning the outcome of the conflict. Within the Pentagon, surface-centric traditionalists on the Army staff blatantly tried to prohibit the use of the word "air campaign" in the official Title V report that the Department of Defense had to submit to Congress. When that didn't work, others argued variously that since the war went so well, Iraq could not have been such a difficult opponent to defeat; and that the four-day ground campaign accomplished what 39 days of air attack could not. Most disgracefully, some sought to dismiss the previous 39 days of air effort altogether and focus only upon G-Day and afterwards. By grandiloquently dubbing the ground campaign "The Hundred Hour War" – as if all before was but a prequel – they effectively (if unintentionally) dishonored the more than 70

Desert Storm proved yet again that a nation that loses its air power cannot prevail in a conventional war against a nation that secures the air. Scenes such as this burnt-out MiG-29A Fulcrum, caught and destroyed on the ground, show that inventory and force structure aren't enough. (DoD)

Coalition aircrew who died in combat or in combat-related flying before G-Day precisely so the ground campaign would proceed as successfully as it did.

Desert Storm and the transformation of air warfare

Eventually, over time, reality seeped in and unified precision aerospace power, together with such practices as having a single Joint Force Air Component Commander and adhering to a Master Attack Plan and an Air Tasking Order (ATO) became accepted not only by the American military establishment, but by NATO and other partner nations as well.

To their great credit, during the build-up to war and the war itself, President George H.W. Bush, PMs Thatcher and Major, and other Coalition national leaders resisted any temptation to insert themselves into military decision-making at the operational and tactical level. Unfortunately, since the time of *Desert Storm* – and beginning as early as the Balkan wars in the former Yugoslavia in 1995–99 – their successors have increasingly returned to the kind of activist leadership John F. Kennedy, Lyndon Johnson, and Robert McNamara pursued with disastrous consequences between 1962 and 1968. *Desert Storm*, compared to what happened afterwards, from Somalia to the Balkans to Afghanistan, Iraq (again), Syria, and Libya, stands as a beacon to restrained political decision-making and mutually respectful political–military relations.

In the broadest sense, *Desert Storm* highlighted the value of precision – in operations, in location, in targeting. Indeed, one can argue that the influence of precision on warfare was, overall, the war's biggest lesson. Attacks were conducted down to the second, and satellite-based navigation ensured that Coalition air, land, and sea forces were aware both of their precise location, and that of their foes as well. In particular, the results of precision attack surprised even those knowledgeable about service programs for laser and electro-optically guided systems.

Less than ten percent of the weapons tonnage expended on Iraq by American airmen were precision munitions such as LGBs, antitank and cruise missiles, and Walleye glide bombs. The LGB, the war's precision weapon stand-out, constituted less than half of this, totaling only 4.3 percent of munitions expended, but was credited afterwards with 75 percent of the serious damage to Iraqi strategic and operational targets. It dominated strategic strikes against leadership and command and control targets, the counter-air campaign against Iraqi airfields, interdiction strikes on bridges and railroads, and battlefield attacks on tanks, artillery, and APCs. One can only imagine how rapidly the course of the Gulf War might have been if, instead of less than ten percent of munitions being precision weapons, particularly LGBs, over 90 percent had been.

That latter figure was, in fact, the percentage of precision munitions expended by American airmen little more than four years later in the late summer of 1995 over the Balkans during Operation *Deliberate Force*, the first time in history that NATO as a treaty organization went to war, against Bosnian Serbian forces in the former Yugoslavia. In that brief conflict, of the total munitions American airmen expended, fully 98 percent were precision ones.

In 1999, precision air power as pioneered in *Desert Storm* saved NATO from what could have been a strategic disaster, perhaps even destroying the alliance in its 50th year. Contradictory, confused, over-optimistic, and inconsistent decision-making by European and American political leaders and the leaders of the United Nations, endangered NATO's efforts to prevent Slobodan Milošević from ethnically cleansing Kosovo. Like Saddam, Milošević believed he could defeat any land-attack by NATO, particularly in the convoluted

The Coalition benefited greatly from the extensive investment in military infrastructure made during the 1980s by the Saudi government. Concerned by Soviet and Iranian aggression, the Royal Saudi Air Force (RSAF) built many large, modern bases. Here, Tornado ADV interceptors from the RSAF's No. 12 Squadron stand on quick reaction alert at Dhahran, home to RSAF and USAF F-15C, RSAF Hawk T. Mk. 65, RSAF Tornado ADV and IDS, and RAF Tornado F.3, GR.1, and GR.1A squadrons. (DoD)

tree-covered terrain of the former Yugoslavia. When, after some weeks, focused, precision air power was unleashed, even though it was more constrained than in *Desert Storm*, it still sufficed to topple the Milošević regime that June. "The capitulation of President Milošević," the late military historian Sir John Keegan wrote, "proved that a war can be won by air power alone."

Desert Storm heralded a new model of war that emphasized the interplay of precision attack systems – aircraft, cruise missiles, helicopters, guided missiles such as the Army's ATACMs, remotely piloted vehicles, etc. – partnering with special operations forces. It heralded as well the arrival of stealth, launching a global interest in "low observable" inhabited and uninhabited systems that continues to this day; signaled the vital importance of increasing the relative percentage of precision attack systems and precision attack weapons in the inventories of the world's air forces and air arms; and encouraged the so-called "drone" revolution that has reshaped modern definitions of combat power in the present day.

Within the United States, after the war, Air Force Secretary Donald B. Rice and then-Chief of Staff Gen Merrill A. "Tony" McPeak reorganized the Air Force's major combatant, logistical, and research and development commands, and reshaped air doctrine and professional military education and training. The Navy reshaped its carrier strike forces to incorporate greater numbers of precision weapons, particularly ones capable of penetrating hardened targets, and, inspired by the F-15E Strike Eagle, transformed the single-purpose F-14A Tomcat into a much more capable swing-role "Bombcat," incorporating LANTIRN so that it could undertake F-15E-level precision attack using laser-guided bombs and, later, the GPS-cued Joint Direct Attack Munitions (JDAM). The Army wisely de-emphasized costly and logistically prohibitive large cannon systems such as the abortive (if technologically highly advanced) Crusader gun system in favor of more practicable rocket-based systems. Looking to its experience attacking fielded forces before the I MEF, the Marine Corps invested more heavily in precision guided weapons.

Nor was the United States alone in defense transformation in the aftermath of *Desert Storm*. Various air leaders around the globe – the NATO nations, the former Eastern European nations of the Warsaw Pact, the ASEAN nations, the Russian Federation, the People's Republic of China, among many others – reorganized and restructured their own combat forces; re-examined and revised their air doctrines; revamped their military education and training structures; and accelerated or initiated efforts to expand or acquire technologies and capabilities showcased in the war, such as precision air-to-surface weapons, cruise missiles, satellite navigation, and radar-confounding "stealth" aircraft. In all of their activities, but especially in doctrine and education, the example and lessons of *Desert Storm*'s focused and precise air power application were uppermost.

Desert Storm by the numbers

As shown in the table (right), overall, Coalition airmen flew 118,661 interdiction; close air support; forward air control; counter-air; airlift; reconnaissance; refueling; special operations; electronic warfare; command, control, and communications (C³), and various miscellaneous sorties. Of these, the United States flew 101,370 sorties, roughly 85 percent; the other Coalition members flew 17,291, roughly 15 percent.

Within just the United States portion of the air campaign, the US Air Force flew 69,406 sorties (68 percent); the US Navy flew 18,303 sorties (18 percent); and the US Marine Corps flew 10,683 sorties (11 percent). The US Army flew 916 sorties (0.90 percent), but this is misleading, as the Army only counts fixed-wing sorties, not rotary-wing ones, which are counted by hours. There were an additional 2,062 sorties (two percent) by CENTCOM's special operations command and by Civil Reserve Air Fleet airmen.

TOTAL SORTIES BY COALITION MEMBERS: 17 JANUARY 1991– 28 FEBRUARY 1991	
Nation	Sorties
Saudi Arabia	6,852
United Kingdom	5,417
France	2,258
Canada	1,302
Kuwait	780
Bahrain	293
Italy	237
United Arab Emirates	109
Qatar	43
United States of America	101,370
USAF	69,406
USN	18,303
USMC	10,683
US Army	916
SOCCENT	1,262
CRAF	800
Coalition total	118,661

Note that US Army totals are for fixed-wing aircraft, as helicopter operations are tracked by flight hours, not sorties.

COALITION PARTNER SORTIES BY MISSION AREA	
Mission	Sorties flown
Air interdiction	38,277
Close air support & forward air control	6,128
Counter-air	23,745
Airlift	22,064
Reconnaissance	3,236
Air refueling	15,895
Special operations	948
Electronic warfare	2,918
Command, control & communications (C3)	1,989
Various miscellaneous sorties	3,461
Total sorties flown	118,661
Note: Airlift includes 800 US CRAF sorties flown during the war.	

AVERAGE DAILY SORTIES FLOWN BY MISSION AREA	
Mission	Average daily sorties flown
Air interdiction	890
Close air support & forward air control	143
Counter-air	552
Airlift	513
Reconnaissance	75
Air refueling	370
Special operations	22
Electronic warfare	68
Command, control & communications (C3)	46
Various miscellaneous sorties	80
Total average daily sorties flown	2,759
Airlift includes 800 US CRAF sorties flown during the war.	

Altogether, as shown (left), roughly 20 percent of Coalition air operations went towards control of the air; another 37 percent covered air-to-surface attack. Airlift and air-refueling, two critical enabling areas, together accounted for approximately 32 percent of Coalition sorties.

As shown (left), on a typical day in *Desert Storm*, Coalition airmen flew an average of 2,759 sorties. The peak sortie day, despite its terrible weather, was Day 39, February 24, "G-Day," the onset of the ground campaign, when Coalition airmen flew 3,280 sorties. The lowest number of sorties occurred on Day 4, January 20, when weather limited sorties to just 2,279. That sortie rates remained so uniform across the war is a tribute to the Coalition maintainers, and also to the robust reliability of the aircraft and engines themselves.

The next table enumerates the Coalition's combat losses over 43 days. Altogether, the Coalition lost 38 aircraft, of which 9 fell to conventional "Triple A," 13 to IR-SAMs, 10 to radar-guided SAMs, 1 to a fighter, 1 to flying into the ground while evading a non-existent threat, and 4 to unknown causes. The majority of losses – at least 23 (60 percent), and possibly 27 (71 percent) – stemmed from low-altitude gun and missile defenses, the latter both IR-missiles and systems such as the SA-3 and the Roland. Had the air campaign not moved to higher altitudes, undoubtedly losses would have been even higher. As they were, they were roughly 38 percent of what Horner, as JFACC, had thought they might be. Not surprisingly, aside from the special case of the RAF's Tornado GR.1, the aircraft that took the greatest losses were those intended for battlefield air support, particularly the A-10A/OA-10A (6 lost) and the AV-8B (five lost).

While *Desert Storm* showcased the devastating leverage of precision-guided munitions, this was hardly a new lesson. Precision air-launched missile warfare dated to 1943 – the Nazi Fritz-X guided glide bomb sank the Italian battleship *Roma* – and featured prominently in the Vietnam War, which marked the debut of the laser-guided bomb. The Navy's Vietnam-era Martin AGM-62B Walleye II glide bomb, which carried a 2,015lb shaped charge warhead returned to combat in the Gulf War, dropped on power stations, communications facilities, bunkers, and command posts, among other targets. (DoD)

Coalition aircraft combat losses										
Nation	Service	Type lost	AAA	IR SAM	Radar SAM	Other	Fighter	Unknown	Number lost
USA	USAF	A-10/OA-10	0	6	0	0	0	0	6
		AC-130	0	1	0	0	0	0	1
		EF-111	0	0	0	1	0	0	1
		F-15E	1	0	1	0	0	0	2
		F-16	1	0	2	0	0	0	3
		F-4G	1	0	0	0	0	0	1
	USN	A-6	2	0	1	0	0	0	3
		F-14	0	0	1	0	0	0	1
		F/A-18	0	0	0	0	1	1	2
	USMC	AV-8B	2	3	0	0	0	0	5
		OV-10	0	2	0	0	0	0	2
S. Arabia	RSAF	F-5	0	0	0	0	0	1	1
		Tornado IDS	1	0	0	0	0	0	1
UK	RAF	Tornado GR.1	1	1	4	0	0	1	7
Italy	AMI	Tornado IDS	0	0	0	0	0	1	1
Kuwait	KuAF	A-4	0	0	1	0	0	0	1
Total coalition losses by cause			9	13	10	1	1	4	38
Source: Data extracted and/or computed from GWAPS v.5: Statistical Compendium, Tables 85–6, 89, 95, 97–100, 104–5, 107, 129–30, 145, 147, 203–4, and 205.									

The table below enumerates the Coalition's human cost in aircrew killed, missing, and taken prisoner. Altogether, the Coalition lost 49 military aviators killed in action (KIA), one missing (later recovered and reclassified as KIA), and approximately 24 killed in operational accidents, raising the total of aviators killed in *Desert Storm* to 74. On top of this, another 30 were captured after ejecting from stricken aircraft or crashed helicopters. Again low altitude – whether from enemy fire or from the dangers inherent in flying fast close to the ground, particularly with indistinct visibility or at night – was particularly dangerous.

Coalition aircrew killed, missing, and taken prisoners of war						
Nation	Service	KIA	MIA	POW	KWF	Total
USA	USAF	20	-	8	3	31
	USN	5	1	3	-	9
	USMC	3	-	5	7	15
	USA	16	-	3	8	27
S. Arabia	RSAF	-	-	1	1	2
UK	RAF	5	-	7	3	15
France	FAF	-	-	-	1	1
Italy	AMI	-	-	2	-	2
Kuwait	KuAF	-	-	1	-	1
Oman	OAF	-	-	-	1	1
Coalition total		49	1	30	24	104
Note: KIA: Killed in Action; MIA: Missing in Action; POW: Prisoner of War; KWF: Killed While Flying (operational loss). The US MIA, Capt Michael Speicher USN, was declared KIA in 2009.						

Plus ça change, plus ça la même chose …

For those who hoped, like President Bush, that the end of the Cold War would usher in a "New World Order," it brought instead the onset of a "New World Disorder," as the first Gulf War, the Balkans, Somalia, Rwanda, Chechnya, Kosovo, 9/11, Afghanistan, and their collective aftermaths, accompanied by a million or so dead, sadly illustrates. New and unexpected dictators and totalitarian states arose, ethnic and religious conflicts continued, and a wave of terrorist attacks (most notably those of September 11, 2001) swept across many lands. Indeed, the shocks and dislocations of the post-Cold War era are really the lingering aftershocks of the true "Mother of All Battles," the (in its time aptly named) "Great War" which, with historical hindsight, must be considered the Peloponnesian War of the modern era, in that it spawned the destruction of the European imperial order, birthed corrosive totalitarian movements that triggered an even more horrendous second global war, and unleashed multiple ideological, nationalistic, and ethnic movements that continue, over a century later, to disorder global comity. Over a century later, we may say with certainty, we are still within the seething world created by those who launched the Great War in 1914, and will be for some time to come.

Desert Storm removed Iraq's ability to assault its neighbors, and must be counted as its singular accomplishment. Focused, precise air power – more properly aerospace power, as much of what Coalition airmen did was only possible because of satellite-furnished communications, weather, navigation, intelligence, and warning – made that victory both swift and, if not blood-free, at least less bloody, for both victor and vanquished. Thereafter, northern and southern "No Fly Zones" kept Saddam's military in the box, punctuated by periodic shoot-downs of Iraqi aircraft and bombings and cruise missile attacks on Iraqi military targets, most notably after an April 1993 attempt by Saddam Hussein to assassinate George H.W. Bush during his post-Presidential visit to Kuwait University.

A dozen years after *Desert Storm*, following reports (some verified but many not) of alleged weapons of mass destruction (WMD), his son, President George W. Bush, supported by Prime Minister Tony Blair, launched the Second Gulf War. This war was even quicker – three weeks rather than six – and toppled the Saddam regime, leading to his capture, trial, conviction for crimes against humanity, and execution. But, given the years of occupation that followed; the steady toll in treasure and those (on all sides) killed and wounded; and the instability and regional disorder that has followed; one finds little satisfaction beyond having ended the brutal reign of Saddam, his sadistic sons, and the Tikriti brotherhood.

One enduring lesson, too little appreciated, is not to go to war without a clear definition of the goals and the desired end-state after the bombing and shooting stops. In *Desert Storm*, President George H.W. Bush, PM Margaret Thatcher, SecDef Richard Cheney, and CENTCOM Gen Norman Schwarzkopf established and pursued a limited goal: get Iraq out of Kuwait. In Operation *Iraqi Freedom*, President George W. Bush, PM Tony Blair, SecDef Donald Rumsfeld, and CENTCOM Gen Tommy Franks went to war with the goal of removing Saddam Hussein from power and ending any programs he had to pursue weapons of mass destruction. But there was precious little thought given to the end-state after Saddam was gone, aside from vague notions of nation-building and infusing democracy into a country (and region) without any previous tradition of it. Their successors, alas, failed equally badly. The result has been a continuing quagmire leaving thousands dead and injured and that is, as of 2021, far from over.

If today's multipolar world is far more uncertain and violent, riven by old and new rivalries, hatreds, and contentions, and the social and societal dislocation and insecurities generated by natural calamities and pandemics, there is some comfort in this: if force is required, the example of *Desert Storm*'s air campaign and the enduring value of joint and combined air power offers assurance that modern precision aerospace power, employed by well-led, well-trained, and courageous aircrew, stands as the most reasonable, effective, and humane means of frustrating global aggressors.

CENTCOM commander Gen H. Norman Schwarzkopf (L) and Saudi Joint Force Commander HRH General Khaled bin Sultan take the salute of Coalition forces. Both men carefully respected the prerogatives and authorities of the other, becoming not only effective and trusting colleagues but very good and lasting friends. The success of the multi-national Coalition can be traced to these two, the architects of victory. (DoD)

FURTHER READING

Allen, Charles. *Thunder and Lightning: The RAF in the Gulf* (Warner Books/HMSO, 1991)

Atkinson, Rick. *Crusade: The Untold Story of the Persian Gulf War* (Houghton Mifflin Company, 1993)

Billière, Gen Sir Peter de la. *Storm Command* (Harper Collins Publishers, 1992)

Bush, President George H.W., and Lt Gen Brent Scowcroft USAF (ret.). A *World Transformed* (Alfred A. Knopf, 1998)

Cheney, Dick, with Liz Cheney. *In My Time* (Threshold Editions, 2011)

Clancy, Tom, and Gen Chuck Horner, USAF (ret.). *Every Man a Tiger* (G.P. Putnam's Sons, 1999)

Comer, Maj Gen Richard, USAF (ret.). "Pave Low Leaders," *Air Commando Journal* 1, no. 1 (Fall 2011)

Cooper, Tom. "The First Night: [The] Iraqi Air Force in Combat – 17 January 1991," *International Air Power Review* 26 (2009).

Deere, Capt David N. (ed.). *Desert Cats* (Fortress Publications/Esprit de Corps Magazine, 1991)

Ehrhardt, Patrick, and Jean-Pierre Hoehn. "Guerre du Golfe: L'oeil du Daguet et la griffe du Jaguar," *Le Fana de l'Aviation,* n. 282 (May 1993)

Freedman, Lawrence, and Efraim Karsh. *The Gulf Conflict, 1990–1991* (Princeton University Press, 1993)

García, Miguel. *Iraqi Mirages in Combat* (Old Iraqi Army Archive, 2018)

Glosson, Lt Gen Buster, USAF (ret.). *War with Iraq: Critical Lessons* (Glosson Family Foundation, 2003)

Hallion, Richard P. *Storm over Iraq: Air Power and the Gulf War* (Smithsonian Institution Press, 1992)

Hallion, Richard P. "Charles A. Horner: Desert Storm Maestro," in Col John Andreas Olsen RNorAF (ed.), *Air Commanders* (Potomac Books, 2013)

Hine, ACM Sir Patrick, RAF. "Despatch by ACM Sir Patrick Hine GCB ADC FRAeS CBIM RAF, Joint Commander of Operation *Granby*, August 1990–April 1991," *The London Gazette,* Second Supplement, No. 52589 (June 28, 1991)

Hooten, E. R., and Tom Cooper. *Desert Storm, Volume 1: The Iraqi Invasion of Kuwait and Operation Desert Shield 1990–1991* (Helion and Co., Ltd 2019)

Hooten, E. R., and Tom Cooper. *Desert Storm, Volume 2: Operation Desert Storm and the Coalition Liberation of Kuwait* (Helion and Co., Ltd 2021)

Jamieson, Perry D. *Lucrative Targets: The USAF in the Kuwaiti Theater of Operations* (USAF History and Museums Program, 2001)

Lambert, Gp Capt Andrew P.N., RAF. *The Psychology of Air Power* (Royal United Services Institute for Defence Studies, 1994)

Mann, Col Edward C. III, USAF. *Thunder and Lightning* (USAF Air University, 1995)

Marolda, Edward J., and Robert J. Schneller Jr. *Shield and Sword: The United States Navy and the Persian Gulf War* (Naval Historical Center, 1998)

Matthews, James K., and Cora J. Holt. *So Many, So Much, So Far, So Fast* (US Department of Defense Joint History Office, 1996)

Mersky, Peter B. *US Marine Corps Aviation Since 1912: Fourth Edition* (Naval Institute Press, 2009)

Micheletti, Eric. *Operation Daguet* (Concord Publications Co., 1991)

Morgan, Rick. *A-6 Intruder Units, 1974–1996* (Osprey Publishing, 2017)

Morin, Maj Jean, and Lt Cdr Richard H. Gimblett. *Operation Friction 1990–1991* (Dundurn Press and Directorate of History of the Department of National Defence, 1997)

Munro, Sir Alan. *Arab Storm* (Tauris & Co., Ltd, 2006 edn)

Napier, Michael. *Tornado GR1: An Operational History* (Pen & Sword Books Ltd, 2017)

Pokrant, Marvin. *Desert Storm at Sea* (Greenwood Press, 1999)

Powell, Gen Colin, USA (ret.) with Joseph E. Persico. *My American Journey* (Random House, 1995)

Putney, Diane. *Airpower Advantage: Planning the Gulf War Air Campaign, 1989–1991* (USAF History and Museums Program, 2004)

Reynolds, Lt Col Richard T., USAF. *Heart of the Storm* (Air University Press, 1995)

Ritchie, Sebastian. "The Royal Air Force and the First Gulf War, 1990–1991," *Air Power Review* 17, no. 1 (Spring 2014)

Schubert, Frank N., and Theresa L. Kraus (eds). *The Whirlwind War* (US Army Center of Military History, 1995)

Schwarzkopf, Gen H. Norman, USA (ret.), with Peter Petre. *It Doesn't Take a Hero* (Bantam Books, 1992)

Sultan, HRH Gen Khaled bin, with Patrick Seale. *Desert Warrior* (Harper Collins Publishers, 1995)

Thatcher, Baroness Margaret. *The Downing Street Years* (Harper Collins Publishers, 1993)

United Kingdom, Royal Air Force. Air Commodore Alistair Byford, RAF. "Operation *Granby* and the Dawn of Precision in the Royal Air Force: A Personal Perspective," *RAF Air Power Review* 21, no. 2 (Summer 2018)

United Kingdom, Royal Air Force. RAF Centre for Air Power Studies. *RAF Air Power Review: First Gulf War 25th Anniversary Special Edition* (Summer 2016)

United Kingdom, Royal Air Force. Gp Capt Andrew G.B. Vallance, RAF. "Air Power in the Gulf War – The RAF Contribution," *Air Clues: The Royal Air Force Magazine* 45, no. 7 (July 1991)

United States, Central Intelligence Agency. *Iraqi Ballistic Missile Developments: An Intelligence Assessment,* CIA SW 90-10045JX (CIA Directorate of Intelligence, July 1990) [Approved for release on June 21, 2011]

United States, Department of Defense [I. Lewis Libby, Report Director, et al.]. *Conduct of the Persian Gulf War: Final Report to Congress Pursuant to Title V of the Persian Gulf Conflict Supplemental Authorization and Personnel Benefits Act of 1991 (Public Law 102-25)* (Government Printing Office, 1992)

United States, Gulf War Air Power Survey [Eliot A. Cohen, Survey Director, et al.]. *Gulf War Air Power Survey, Summary Report* and volumes 1–5 (Government Printing Office, 1993)

Whitcomb, Col Darrel D., USAF (ret.). *On a Steel Horse I Ride* (USAF Air University Press, 2012)

Winnefeld, RADM James A., USN (ret.), Preston Niblack, and Dana J. Johnson. *A League of Airmen* (The RAND Corporation, 1994)

Witts, Gp Capt Jeremy, RAF. "Tornado GR.1 – the Gulf – Training and Tactics," *Royal Air Force Historical Society Journal* 20 (1999)

Woods, Kevin M. *Iraqi Perspectives Project Phase II – Um Al-Ma'arik (The Mother of All Battles),* v. 1 (Institute for Defense Analyses, May 2008)

Woods, Kevin M., Williamson Murray, and Thomas Holaday with Mounir Elkhamri. *Saddam's War* (US National Defense University, 2009)

INDEX